Lessons from an Ice Cream Truck

Pineapple....XVI

Lessons from an Ice Cream Truck
All Rights Reserved.
Copyright © 2014 Pineapple....XVI
v2.0

Cover Photo © 2014 Pineapple....XVI. All rights reserved - used with permission.

Outskirts Press, Inc.
http://www.outskirtspress.com

ISBN: 978-1-4787-3201-3

Outskirts Press and the "OP" logo are trademarks belonging to
Outskirts Press, Inc.

PRINTED IN THE UNITED STATES OF AMERICA

outskirtspress
DENVER, COLORADO

Contents

Welcome to the economy.

Many children experience their first usage of money, while purchasing ice cream from a truck. There have been many times in which parents have taught their children how to calculate change while receiving their treats from me. There was a particularly interesting situation one time with a young girl whose age was about seven years, in which after she and her friends chose their ice cream, she handed me a ten dollar bill and started to walk away. The total for the four items was six dollars. I told her to wait a second to receive her change. She replied, "I never used money before, I don't know how it works."

The truck I drive has signs on it which say, "WATCH CHILDREN" and "WATCH THAT CHILD". It seems that everyone who receives ice cream from me is a kid. Some of those kids are a lot older than 18. The very young people usually get a small popsicle. A few young children have approached the truck without knowledge of all the fancy items it carries. They possessed knowledge of one thing though, and have said three words to convey their desire: "I want chocolate." Their older sibling or parent then buys them a fudge bar. Many of the older people would like the truck to carry beverages which are available at a saloon.

I travel around many places, far more than most ice cream truck drivers. Most other drivers cruise around a city over and over. Some of them visit the same streets and neighborhoods repeatedly during a week.

I don't follow that plan.

The ice cream trucks I have driven start as regular vans purchased brand new by my boss, Bob. Bob has been in the ice cream business over 40 years. The new van has lights and signs added to it, and unless it's a Dodge Sprinter, has a turtle top installed to make it taller. A speaker is added to the front, with an electronic music box installed to send signals to it. A Nelson freezer is added which is specifically designed to be used as a mobile freezer. The truck is plugged in at night to keep the freezer cold. Nelson freezers have special steel plates to maintain the cold temperature as the truck drives around all day. Sometimes, extreme circumstances arise which necessitate the use of dry ice. Dry ice is 109 degrees below zero Fahrenheit, and keeps the ice cream VERY cold during those occasional situations.

Mister Frosty is the place where about 36 ice cream trucks are parked at night, and loading of the ice cream occurs. Some of the truck maintenance occurs here also. Semi-trucks bring loads of ice cream to be stored in the giant freezers until needed by the ice cream truck drivers.

Bob owns about half the trucks and the ice cream inside them. Eddie owns the other trucks parked at Mister Frosty. Bob employs two dock workers to transfer ice cream to and from the freezers. As a driver, I provide fuel for the truck, which allows me to drive wherever I want. My time is not payed for. My income is entirely a straight percentage of each day's sales that I make. I have had a few days which ended with negative income because my fuel expense was greater than my sales percentage. Some of my days also produced very low amounts of money after 7 or 8 hours of driving around. I am able to survive on a low income due to being single with no children to support.

The other trucks at Mister Frosty are required to be there every night within an hour after dusk. The truck I drive is exempt from that rule because I have proven to Bob that I can give him more money by doing things the **Pineapple....XVI** way.

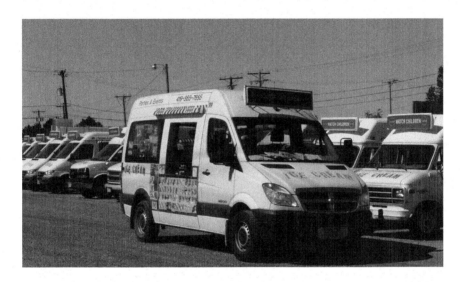

I began my life as an ice cream man when I noticed the big sign,

"DRIVERS WANTED".

I was looking for another delivery job because I **LOVE** to drive.

I have been employed as a delivery man by many companies. I have been collecting maps since I was 16 and love to develop routes for efficient travel or scenic pleasure. Two of my grandparents were self-employed involving retail sales, but I don't think of my job as trying to sell ice cream. I like to think that I get paid by just driving around.

There have been a few times in which my sales instincts paid off.

I didn't earn much money the first two seasons because I didn't know where to drive. I drove around the city too much and occasionally went to a neighboring county. As a new driver who didn't sell much ice cream, Bob didn't always have a truck for me to drive. His more experienced drivers made more money for him. He wanted me to be able to work and gain experience though. He would check with Eddie to see if he needed a driver on those days. Eddie was happy when Bob didn't have a truck for me on the day of my Kalida fireworks show the first year.

In my third year, my ice cream horizons changed dramatically.

My natural love of exploration began to pay off in many ways. I was able to expand my knowledge of the rural landscape and meet lots of new people. I love to participate in the excitement of ice cream truck rookies. It might be considered a financial gamble to spend so much fuel to explore new areas so far from home, but I am always rewarded by being able to make someone happy with the opportunity to buy ice cream from a truck.

Some of my driving strategies relate to a friend's comment about me being the ice cream man. I take that role seriously and consider it my responsibility to find that next person who needs the positive emotions which an ice cream truck provides.

Many times, customers are few and far between, and my extensive amounts of driving seem more like pro bono work. I don't drive an ice cream truck to become a millionaire though. In the grand scheme of things, I earn a few dollars and I'm adding smiles to our world.

At the beginning of my second season, I started wearing a spider hat while driving around distributing ice cream. I bought the hat a few years before that, because I like spiders and the two colors of the hat are used by my favorite sports team. Customers immediately responded in a positive way to my hat. The other ice cream truck drivers started calling me, "Spidey".

Customers frequently offered to buy the hat from me, for more than double what I paid for it.

I went back to the store I bought it from, but they no longer sold hats. Ice cream customers develop a loyalty to their ice cream man. If they've bought ice cream from the same person a few times on a regular basis, they shun other ice cream truck drivers. My loyal customers could easily identify me by the spider hat on my head.

Occasionally, during very hot weather, I would take it off and discovered that customers were disappointed by its absence. There was an occasion where upon reaching a new stop for the third time, a young girl asked me if I knew Pineapple 16. I grabbed the hat, put it on, and the girl was happy that Pineapple was suddenly there to sell her ice cream.

One day I was driving to a friend's house, before starting my route; I didn't have my spider hat on yet. She lives in a rural area which is not likely to be frequented by ice cream trucks. I was on my way to drop something off for her. Less than one mile from her house, we passed each other on the road, going opposite directions. She didn't know I was on my way but noticed an ice cream truck coming toward her; an ice cream truck is hard to miss. I was surprised that she didn't stop. I turned around and caught up with her to give her the item. She said, "I didn't know it was you; you aren't wearing your spider hat."

I like to think of my spider hat as my ice cream truck uniform.

I grew up near the small town of Oak Harbor, Ohio on a road which only has a 55 MPH speed limit. That road is only half a mile from town and had many young people on the half mile section near my house. An ice cream truck should have been exploring it. I love to explore new towns and prefer them to not be big enough to need a stoplight. I also realize that the desire to buy ice cream from a truck is stronger in rural areas than in the city. In 2008, I sold ice cream to people in 51 different counties. The number of counties has increased each year since then as my horizons keep stretching farther apart.

Since my childhood was devoid of ice cream truck activity, I was unaware of my special role in society as an ice cream man. I was quickly made aware of its significance after telling my friend Warren about my new job. His exuberant response of, "**YOU'RE THE ICE CREAM MAN !?**" told me a lot. The key word in his response is "the".

I soon learned from many customers, that I am not **AN** ice cream man; I am **THE** ice cream man.

Behavior Modification

I have noticed many ways in which the ice cream truck modifies the behavior of citizens it is near. I enjoy observing the power and persuasion that the truck possesses.

I have seen people suddenly start dancing as I drove by. Some of the people who approach the truck are giddy in a way which would cause others to believe intoxicants were involved. Countless people go out of their way to wave at me. It's cute when a small child waves at me and I notice their joy as I wave back. Some of their waves seem ritualistic like a salute to a superior officer. I have seen people run to their front door just to wave as I went by. There have been many times in which passengers in a car in front of me at a red light turn around in unison to see me.

It's obvious that the driver noticed an ice cream truck in their rearview mirror and then told them. They usually wave.

I enjoy the sociological study of people affected by decisions they must make when choosing which ice cream novelty to buy.

The variety of people and their financial situations vary greatly. Their desires are greeted by over sixty different items in the freezer. Of course the people with plenty of money to spend have all the items to choose from, if their dietary restrictions are not a factor. Some people have food allergies or are diabetic.

The multitude of options are too much for some people to handle. I occasionally get asked for suggestions. I ask if they want ice cream or a popsicle. I ask if they want chocolate or something fruity. I point out my three favorite items. I describe the Big Bopper ice cream sandwich as the only thing on the truck better than the driver.

The people with limited financial resources sometimes exhibit behaviors which are otherwise not seen by me; there are pros and cons for me in those situations. I greatly dislike the amount of time used by the conflict between parents and their children over the expenditure of one dollar, or less.

If the truck were suddenly removed from the scene, a random witness listening to the conversation, might conclude from the child's comments that the decisions about to be made are extremely critical, with potential consequences leading to life-altering results.

Many times a parent will limit their child to one or two dollars, but the child wants an item which costs three dollars. Some children have their will tested, and their level of stubbornness sometimes affects the end result. Sometimes the end result is that they get nothing. Sometimes their desire for sugar from the ice cream truck trumps their stubbornness and they accept the cheaper item. Of course I prefer to sell higher-priced items. I also prefer the consumer be able to obtain their favorite choice, however, I love to witness the surrender with the knowledge that the child just received a lesson in economics.

One of the things which bothers me is when a parent restricts a child's purchase based on the price while allowing them to buy a different item which costs the same amount. The parent is comparing value or frivolity with an ice cream purchase, which seems ridiculous to me.

My financial situation is improved with every purchase a customer makes. When adults deny themselves a delicious cold treat because of being stingy, I don't care about the loss of my potential commission.

One time while stopped on a road under repair, the flagman looked at the menu and commented that he can get the item he wanted at a much cheaper price. I replied, "Not on this road."

He responded, "You got me there."; he bought the item from me.

Clothing Optional

Depending on the frequency which an ice cream truck appears, people's behavior can exhibit different results. The urgency of the situation for those wanting to buy ice cream has caused three different women to run out to the street wearing nothing but a towel.

One of those women was a regular customer whom I would see every Monday for two years. She was about 30 and very attractive. She lived on a farm with a driveway that went around behind the house. She usually came out of the house within eight seconds of my arrival. On that particular Monday, I arrived at about my usual time with the music playing. I slowly circled the house, but she didn't appear. I left her property as she exited the shower. She heard the ice cream music just as I continued down the road. She ran out to the middle of the road wearing her towel and waving her arms. I failed to check my mirrors at that time, which the following Monday I regretted, after she told me what had happened.

The other two women were students at one of the universities I drive near. They were roommates and were preparing to go out for the evening. I don't know if they were pre-shower or post-shower, but when I drove by, they each ran out of their house while only wearing a towel. It was dark out with no pedestrian traffic on their block. They both ran out of their house screaming, "**Wait !! ice cream truck !**" Another roommate of theirs ran out with them and had money for their purchases. Their absence of clothes did not deter them from experiencing a visit to the ice cream truck.

Shortly after I started selling ice cream at night, I drove by a man and woman walking in downtown Toledo. There were no other pedestrians on the block where I encountered them. The ice cream truck was the only vehicle traveling the street on that block at that time. To get my attention, the man yelled, "**Hey ice cream man !**" I started slowing down to stop as I turned my head to see him. They were walking toward the area in which I had just traveled as the woman pulled her own shirt and bra up for a few seconds. They had no intention of buying ice cream, but for me, it was one of my favorite non-customer encounters.

Another of my favorite non-customer encounters came while in the town of Ostrander, Ohio. There have been dozens of times in various places and situations where a child or children will start jumping and screaming as the ice cream truck approaches them. My immediate reaction is to slow down or stop to see if they're buying ice cream. Sometimes an older child or adult will signal me to keep driving.

I love it when they help my efficiency by communicating that they are not buying anything. The situation in Ostrander which I loved, occurred as I approached the baseball diamond and several children began jumping and screaming. I then noticed a man signaling to me the same way that a third base coach signals to a runner to keep going to home plate. I would have loved to sell the children some ice cream, but I thoroughly enjoyed the man's communication to me that they were not buying. I was laughing pretty good as I kept driving.

There have been several times in which children have heard the ice cream music coming toward them, and ran into their house screaming hysterically in such a way, that their parents or grandparents thought someone broke their arm, or other tragedy happened.

The adult would tell me their reaction after coming out to the truck to pay for the ice cream. The places where that situation has happened have been in areas where another ice cream truck has probably never been. The locations were not far from typical ice cream routes though.

The children were familiar with ice cream trucks existing in their area, but NOT in THEIR rural neighborhood.

Due to my habit of driving quickly, I have seen many people run out of their house to catch me. I also have seen people in my mirrors after I drive by. They are standing in the middle of the road waving their arms. When I started going to the village of Clinton, one of the families asked me when I would return. I told them I would be back the following Tuesday. One week later, as I went around the curve of their street with their house in visual range, I noticed the family standing by the curb waiting for me. That was an unusual sight for me. Since their dead-end street is at the edge of Clinton, I wondered how much of the ice cream music had saturated their neighborhood before my arrival.

After I stopped, I asked them how long they had been waiting for me.

The mom replied, "Since you were here last week."

When I drive in areas completely devoid of ice cream truck activity, many of the residents exhibit various reactions. Two of my summer road trips took me to northern Michigan. Several non-customers applauded or gave a thumbs-up gesture as I drove by. I believe that some of them thought that a new ice cream route had been created and they would start seeing the truck on a regular basis.

When another road trip took me to Minnesota, I saw dozens of people who were completely stunned. Some of them looked to me as if they were watching a U.F.O. float by. I saw several adults stop the vehicle they were driving to watch me drive by. I noticed many jaws drop farther than I had ever seen before. I'm glad that my friend Tami was with me to notice the recurring reaction.

On the way to Tami's in northern Minnesota, I drove by one side of Otter Tail Lake. A VERY rare situation occurred there, in which during two consecutive stops, people came out to the street to buy ice cream from me, **while holding and eating ice cream.**

I have seen several children and college students react to the presence of the ice cream truck by yelling and running toward the street for a few seconds with no intention of buying ice cream. It has sometimes appeared to be an example of Pavlov's Response.

I enjoy watching dogs confined by invisible fences exhibiting the same response. Some of the dogs respond to the ice cream music as a threat, while others see a potential playmate. Some of the dogs want to race me, just like young boys on a bicycle. The dog will wait at the corner of their yard for me to reach the same longitude or latitude and proceed to race me as I drive by, until they reach the other edge of their yard along the road.

Another thing I have noticed about dogs with the many delivery jobs I've had, is that their behavior typically falls into one of two categories.

When a person they don't know approaches on foot or in a vehicle, they either react with overwhelming friendliness, or demonstrate an intense protective stance. There was an instance where I noticed a dog react to the truck driving by in the same way I've noticed many humans respond. The reaction is pure astonishment.

It's a great joy for me to give many people the opportunity to buy ice cream from a truck. When I drive down roads in extreme rural isolated places, where people have never seen an ice cream truck, they are shocked by my presence. Their typical behavior is to stand there in awe, because they probably didn't even think about the fact, that they never saw an ice cream truck on their road before.

Sometimes there's a darker demonstration of behavior exhibited by members of the general public when specifically encountered by an ice cream truck. I have many times heard young men yell towards the truck with words which reference criminal behavior.

Their belligerence is accentuated by the time of day and location of the typical occurrence. Their remarks usually refer to children even though my encounters with these men occur after children are in bed. Alcohol may have added to the occurrence sometimes, but not always.

Other darker elements of people's behavior are described in the "Dark Side" chapter.

The Chase

Another way in which I've seen people's behavior affected is where they intentionally fail to catch me. I've seen many children, who are usually boys aged 7-12, start to chase me and then when I slow down to allow them to catch me, they stop. I then realize they are not buying ice cream and when I start driving away, they continue chasing me as part of their game.

One time while I was driving near Bowling Green State University, a pair of college girls requested that I drive away at a speed which would allow them the opportunity to chase me without catching me. They had no interest in buying ice cream; they just wanted the experience of chasing me, while yelling at me to wait.

I have been chased for miles by people who wanted ice cream. I've been chased by people driving cars, lawnmowers, bicycles, golf carts, and all-terrain vehicles. People in many different age groups have chased me on foot. People scream, wave their arms, flash lights, and do whatever else they can think of, to get me to stop. I've had two occurrences of a police officer in a small town stopping me to ask if I could go back to a house where a kid wanted ice cream.

One time a police officer approached the truck as I was about to leave a stop in a very small town. He was very serious as he asked if I had the proper paperwork and vending permits. As I turned to get the papers from their location, he smacked his hand on the serving counter and said, "I'm messin' with ya; I just want an ice cream cone."

There were several times in which strangers gave me money and then sent me to an address, to give ice cream to the people at that location.

Sometimes I was given instructions to give the recipient any change; other times I was told to keep the change as a tip. Customers have also called people living miles away to see if I should go there next.

One of Mister Frosty's dock workers supplied a friend with a few ice cream novelties at a discount. I randomly stopped at the friend's house and his son Vince ordered one of the items from me.

Vince's dad told him, "We already have those in the freezer."

Vince replied, "**I want it from the truck !**"

I had other occurrences similar to that. The power of the ice cream truck makes me think that I could drive it to the beach and sell sand.

Another person whose behavior is modified by the ice cream truck is me. When driving any other vehicle, my attention is primarily on the road ahead with occasional glances of my mirrors. I enjoy viewing scenery when possible, but it's casual. People who want ice cream are everywhere. Since I travel to many places which rarely experience ice cream trucks, I need to watch for those people. If I miss them, they might never have that opportunity again.

I've been complimented many times from customers on my ability to spot them. I've seen them over 600 feet away while driving over 40 MPH. The big reason that I have to visually focus on potential customers, is because I usually have Techno music inside the truck, to slightly distract me from the ice cream music outside the truck. Unless my cellular telephone is on maximum volume, I do not hear it.

I often don't hear it anyway.

When I drive in the city at night, I usually have the ice cream music at a lower volume. Since many night parties are in garages or back yards,

I have to drive very slowly. As I scout for possible customers, I feel as if I'm a police officer on patrol looking for criminal activity.

People have joked about mothers having eyes in the back of their heads. There have been times at night in which I thought I was switching to stealth mode by turning off the music and shutting off the canopy lights. Stealth mode only works with adults. Children KNOW an ice cream truck is near.

If I am driving too fast for an adult to get my attention, I take comfort in the idea that they probably can drive to a store to buy sugary treats. I want to avoid causing a child to experience the disappointment of missing the ice cream truck. The sensation of my spider hat on my head, heightens my attention to everything outside the truck. It creates a behavioral change in me which enhances the focus of my responsibility as the ice cream man.

As my attention is focused, I sometimes interpret other environmental factors to be potential customers. My peripheral vision has detected statues of humans with an arm raised, causing me to briefly slow down for a better look.

One of the Techno songs frequently played on my iPod contains two lyrical moments which I have interpreted as a kid yelling for me to stop. After a few times of hearing the song and briefly slowing down, I remembered those moments in the song.

Another sound I have heard, sounds like a kid yelling, "**WAIT**".

I have only encountered it about seven times when driving in rural areas. I'm usually traveling over 50 MPH, when I suddenly hear, "**wayyyt**".

I vigorously apply the brakes and stop.

I turn all the music down to better hear the plea, and usually hear it again, "**wayyyt**". I start looking around for a kid to be running toward the truck waving their arms. When this situation occurs, I have never seen the kid, so I start slowly backing up. Every time this has occurred, there has been zero traffic.

As I get closer to the audio source, I hear it again, "**wayyyt**". As I scan the area for that kid I thought I heard, I discover the source of the plea; it's a peacock.

On June 14, 2010, I was stopped for the third time by a peacock. On that occasion, his owners noticed an ice cream truck backing up slowly in front of their house. They quickly ran out of the front door to stop me. They asked what I was doing. I told them that their peacock stopped me. They were glad, because they wanted to buy ice cream. Mr. Peacock then posed for me.

The few peacocks who stopped me after that, made me smile as the memory of June 14th came back.

I have gotten better at quickly identifying false indicators of potential sales situations.

Another way in which my behavior has been affected by my role as an ice cream man, occurs when I'm not in the truck. I do it while traveling to places I am unlikely to return to. Even though I have experimented with ice cream routes far outside of northwest Ohio, I am highly unlikely to drive an ice cream truck in Hawai'i.

Even though I was thoroughly enjoying the scenery of the Aloha State, I analyzed its ice cream route potential.

I also did that in Tanzania while on a medical mission. I suggested to the team leader the idea that a medical vehicle drive slowly through the rural areas announcing its capabilities instead of us just camping out in one village for four days. We rode for 3 1/2 hours on rough unpaved roads, so we weren't traveling any faster than I drive the ice cream truck.

I have learned that:

Ice cream trucks greatly affect the mood and behavior of people in all age groups. The effects are not always positive.

Some people greatly respect the safety issues with children, that arise when an ice cream truck is stopped. Sadly, I have seen many people, including police officers, ignore the possibility that a child could suddenly run across the street from a blind spot created by the truck I drive.

For many people, most activities are superseded in priority by an ice cream truck.

60 Degrees and Sunny

Weather is a prominent factor with ice cream truck sales. The title I chose for this chapter is from a quote to me from Bob. He said to me,

"60 and sunny is better than 70 and cloudy". I kept that quote in mind during many days of less-than-ideal weather. I believe that for ice cream truck sales, the best weather is 83 degrees and mostly sunny. Higher temperatures cause more people to be inside with air conditioning, with a greater inability to be aware of my presence. On more than one occasion, I heard a woman tell her children to hurry up so they could get back inside away from the heat. Temperatures in the low 80s allow people to have fun outdoors without being too hot. It's warm enough though to be highly seduced by the refreshing satisfaction that ice cream or popsicles provide.

The effects of cooler temperatures depend on the temperature of the previous day. In the spring when midwesterners still have fresh memories of the cold winter, then 46 (8 Celsius) degrees feels warm. I had good sales more than once when the temperature was 46 degrees and sunny in April. If it's only 46 degrees in July, then sales will be very poor.

When heat waves occur, sales are affected negatively. I was interviewed by Toledo's FOX affiliate for a news story about a Toledo heat wave a few years ago. Most people believe that heat waves are good for ice cream truck sales. That myth was discussed in my televised interview.

I mentioned that my strategy includes finding construction workers.

People who are working in an environment without air conditioning are excited about my arrival. They buy a lot of Bomb Pops. I also do my Amish route when it's very hot.

One of Mister Frosty's regular business clients calls to have us show up for an event when the temperature is above 90 (32 C.) degrees. They have about 50 employees working in an air conditioned office. I am perplexed as to why they choose to specifically come out into the heat to enjoy ice cream treats. Personally I prefer 90 degrees, but most people don't like it that hot.

The beginning of the ice cream truck season is greatly affected by the weather. Bob likes to wait for the forecast to show more than a few good consecutive days. Insurance for ice cream trucks is not cheap. If a couple good weather days happen, followed by a week of typical springtime rain, then that's wasted insurance for a parked truck. During my tenure as an ice cream man, my first sales day of the season has varied from March 27th to April 11th. Two of my seasons saw mid-October because of great autumn weather.

In 2011, two of my April weekends were in Columbus, because it was 26-30 degrees Fahrenheit warmer there, compared to Toledo.

I saw my sister's family a lot that spring.

Bob's quote to me about the cloudiness became more prominent as I repeatedly saw its effect.

The temperature is not as important as the absence of clouds.

Rain is typically bad for sales. During one of my return trips from Columbus, it was raining all day. I have several routes between Toledo and Columbus with many repeat customers. On the day it was raining, I only attempted to see customers in one place. It was a small community in Seneca County. Most of the customers I usually saw there were preteen boys. I knew that they wouldn't care that it was raining.

Nights in Bowling Green are also less affected by rain. One night in B.G. it was 53 degrees and pouring rain. Sales were decent.

Depending on my location at the time rain shows up, my alternate plans vary. If I'm far from Toledo, I look for blue skies to possibly keep selling. If I'm near Toledo, I will go to a movie or to the library to wait out the storm. One of my fireworks shows far from Toledo which got hit by rain caused me to go to McDonald's. I used my iPod connected to their Wi-Fi to find another fireworks show that same day farther from Toledo.

One year on Memorial Day, I was enjoying the good sales near Lake Erie and the Sandusky Bay. When I noticed rain approaching, I called Brenda. She is Bob's secretary. After she informed me of the weather pattern, I headed to Columbus, where the weather was gorgeous. I spent that night at my sister's.

Since rain is typically bad for sales, it's great that my willingness to explore other areas to escape it, has paid off.

Rain caused my first ice cream trip to Chicago, and my first ice cream trip to Iowa.

Rain caused me to discover my best sales event location ever.

Those positive results are discussed later in this book.

I have learned that:

Some people want ice cream no matter what the weather is like.

Watching the forecast is helpful, but stay open-minded. Weather patterns change quickly.

Driving in heavy rain causes the loud speaker to not function properly. Its volume is greatly reduced when it gets a little water inside the cone. It must be loosened and drained.

I must be flexible with my route plans because Mother Nature does not care.

Regulars

When I started driving the truck, I had to guess where to find customers. When people asked about when I was returning, I realized that it's a lot easier to sell ice cream when you know where people are, who definitely want to buy some. If I were in a neighborhood which I liked when people asked about my return, I made sure to keep that location in mind. I typically remember every building I have ever delivered anything from my multitude of delivery jobs. Most delivery jobs involve a predetermined delivery address and numbers are easy for me to remember. As my ice cream routes expanded, I was more likely to get requests for return visits. Sometimes I can tell that a delivery point would be a good place to revisit due to customer excitement or other factors, such as high percentage of residents showing interest.

As a season progresses, it's great to have regulars, due to random stops becoming less frequent. One of the tricky aspects is knowing how often to visit each regular customer. During my first several years in the ice cream truck, I drove Friday through Tuesday. I started to develop regular routes for Monday, Tuesday and Friday. I would alternate my Saturdays and Sundays between different routes. Some customers love once a week visits. Some regulars don't want the truck as often.

It becomes a highly strategic plan to create and drive routes which allow the best symbiotic relationship between the customer's desire for ice cream and my need to have fuel paid for.

I have enjoyed developing relationships with regular customers. I have become friends on facebook with many of them. They enjoy seeing my many photographs online relating to my ice cream adventures as well as my many other adventures.

I also post travel plans on facebook allowing the customers to know when I am likely to be in their area. I've been invited into the homes of some of them to see whatever they wanted to show me. I've been invited to join them for meals. Some of my regulars and I have each other's telephone number which has been very useful in different circumstances.

Some regulars have become friends with whom I've spent time with outside of our ice cream relationship. I also receive bonus information about other potential sales opportunities which is more reliable than info from a stranger.

Sometimes regular customers move during our ongoing relationship. One regular has lived five different places in three different counties during my tenure as their ice cream man. Since we have each other's telephone number, we've been able to maintain our ice cream relationship.

One of my regulars whom I usually see every Tuesday, moved during the off-season. Tim and his children live in a city which is far bigger than I prefer to visit. I enjoyed going there several years ago, but my preference for driving locations has changed a lot. Tim is one of my best customers. I typically only have one or two other stops in his city and have kept his city on my route because of him. After discovering that Tim and his family no longer lived in the house where I had seen them for several years, I tried calling him, but he left his telephone at work on that first Tuesday of my new season. Luckily, while leaving in his city that day, I drove near enough to their new neighborhood, that they heard the ice cream music. Tim and his children jumped into their car and they chased me down. He then informed me of their new address.

Some regulars are people at work. Fridays help great sales opportunities. The end of the work week and potentially pay day, puts more people in the mood to enjoy the simple celebration of an ice cream truck experience. Many of the business locations have a receptionist who informs the other employees upon my arrival. I learn patterns of which items are more popular at certain locations.

Some regulars brag to their friends that I know their usual ice cream treat. I enjoy being able to have their usual item ready as they approach the serving window. A few regulars mix it up by trying different items.

Some regulars are not able to buy ice cream from me once a week, or even twice a month. Many of them live far away from Toledo. I have regular customers whom I've only seen once a year for many years. The once-a-year regulars are typically because of fireworks. Some regulars started out as once-a-year due to their distance from Toledo or because of fireworks, but then I started going to some areas a few more times a year. Some buy many items because they know it will be a long time until they see me again.

The Bubble Gum popsicle is NOT available in any store. You can only acquire it from an ice cream truck. Some customers have researched that information and when an ice cream truck goes by, they purchase more than one. One of my regulars started buying many Bubble Gum popsicles from me on an annual basis during one of my fireworks routes. The woman in her 30s told me that she searched online for them and could not find them.

After discussing that situation with Bob, he told me that Blue Bunny makes several items which they only sell to ice cream truck operators.

A few years later, while in a small village located in a different county which I visit a few times a year, a man in his 30s bought many Bubble Gum popsicles. I told him about the woman I used to see once a year. He informed me that she is his wife. He was about to mention it because he recognized my spider hat. It's nice that they moved a little closer to their popsicle supply.

Another regular customer LOVES the Malt Cup. It's also only available from an ice cream truck; it comes with a wooden spoon. I only see that customer about twice a year. During 2013, both visits were in September. Since the Malt Cup is not as popular as many other items, its availability is limited at the end of the season. When I knew that I was going to the area where Malt Cup-lover lives, I told Bob that I need the Malt Cups from the other trucks. My customer bought every Malt Cup I was carrying during both visits. He always wants the wooden spoon too.

One of my regulars is a donkey. Clyde lives near Defiance, Ohio.

I wandered down a road near Clyde one day several years ago. His friend Sherri used to live in Toledo and enjoyed visits from the ice cream truck. When she and her husband moved to a rural area, she thought she would never see an ice cream truck again. Sherri's reaction to my first visit is among my favorite memories. I occasionally am able to get two or three more stops near Sherri's road, but she made it clear that she will ALWAYS want to make a purchase. If she weren't home, then her husband would buy something for her. After several visits to Sherri, she told me about Clyde. She wanted to buy ice cream for Clyde who lives two miles away. Clyde usually spends his time in the back of his pasture which is wooded. When he hears the ice cream music, he comes running, loudly conveying his desire, "HEE HAW HEE HAW". Sherri always buys him a vanilla ice cream cone. He LOVES it. Two times, she also bought him a Bomb Pop. During the second visit of receiving both items, we discovered that he was probably experiencing brain-freeze. He only gets one item now. A popular video on my Youtube channel is the one showing Clyde running for ice cream.

Another regular customer is the Sharp Family. They have a huge family reunion the same weekend every year. They live in an area which I only visit about four times a year. I randomly drove by their house in

2006. The reunion was the following weekend. They made it sound like I should definitely be there; they were right. They have varied their preference for the time of my arrival, but it always works out. All the children in their large family have learned over the years about organizing themselves in a way which makes my visit smooth for everyone involved.

A family I visited every Monday evening several years ago for two seasons, had four boys who always bought something. Three of the boys usually chose something different during each visit. The oldest who was about 16 always bought a Cherry Twin Pop. I was informed by their mother near the end of the first season, that her freezer was loaded with Cherry Twin Pops. Her son enjoyed buying them, but never ate them.

Brittany and Brianna are sisters and have been regulars for many years. They live in a VERY small community of about sixteen houses. My first encounter with them involved being chased by their mom in her car. After she caught me, she told me that I should visit once a week. The two sisters each receive the same amount of money during all my visits. The total has had variances. They always spend every quarter. If their ice cream doesn't use all their money, they buy candy. Occasionally their parents get ice cream too. Sometimes I have shown up and the girls weren't there. Their dad would ask me what their usual items were and then buy them.

Alan and Anna are siblings. They live in a rural area on a dead-end road. Their road only has three houses and their house is at the end of a long lane, which is longer than the public road. I have been driving in their neighborhood for many years. They missed me during my first attempt at trying their road because of their lane being so long. The following year, when I tried their road again, their dad used his golf cart to speed down their lane and out to the opposite end of their road to get my attention right before I entered the main highway. I have seen them once a week for a few seasons now. Alan always buys a

Sno-cone. Anna mixes it up.

Another regular is Chery's daycare center. I have been stopping at Chery's daycare almost every week of the season for over eight years. The children line up and place their order and then sit in the yard to enjoy their treats. Sometimes they yell, "Thank you" in unison as I'm leaving.

Most of my regulars only see one ice cream man. A few of them have other ice cream truck opportunities and choose to only buy their ice cream from me. I appreciate the loyalty they demonstrate.

Some regulars continue to enjoy my visits after years of our relationship. Some of them only last one or two years. At the beginning of each season, I concentrate on serving the regulars first.

Routes are thick with customers early in the season. During the end of each season, I rarely see people who aren't regulars, other than campus crowds.

Some of the college crowds contain students who are regulars, however, I only see them in the spring or autumn.

My weekly customers and I share with each other schedule variations when they arise. I tell them about my road trips or other circumstances which will cause them to not see me the following week. They inform me if they're going to be gone. The ones that know they're going to move tell me their new address. The one who has lived in different counties was surprised during the first move that I could still serve her family, because she didn't know how far my routes go out from Toledo.

An enjoyable scene for me, which the ice cream truck has created, is the meeting of neighbors. Random stops of mine have brought neighbors together as they visit the truck. I especially love it when they are meeting for the first time. I have witnessed a few regulars meet their new neighbor as they came out to buy ice cream from me.

One of my favorite meetings to see was while I was in West Virginia, on a winding rural road. As I was stopped at the house of a customer, a man and his daughter pulled up behind me in a pickup truck and stopped to get ice cream. The man who just arrived went to high school with the man at the house I was in front of. They had not seen each other for almost twenty years. After their kids bought their ice cream treats, I left as the two men were reminiscing about fun times which occurred decades ago.

I have learned that:

Having regular customers is important for helping to maintain a healthy sales consistency.

Regular customers appreciate the service of having an ice cream truck show up in their driveway, or wait for them near it.

Some of them brag to their friends about it.

Some regulars place my participation in their life very high on their priority list.

Having regulars helps aspects of my life outside of the ice cream truck.

Know Your Audience

To successfully operate an ice cream truck, it's good to realize that the truck is part of the entertainment industry as much, or more than being part of the food service industry. Great entertainers know their audience. They know their ages; they know their preferences; they know when their audience wants them; they know when their audience craves them. They also know to leave their audience wanting more.

I know that some of my audience here is other ice cream truck drivers. Since I have not discontinued driving an ice cream truck yet, I will not share every sales strategy I possess. I hope this book helps many people understand ice cream trucks a little better.

When I drive in an area which I know will be more heavily populated with preteen children, it's better to be more heavily stocked with Sno-cones and face popsicles. If I'm headed to a car show, then ice cream cones, ice cream bars, and ice cream sandwiches are in higher demand. I have learned that certain geographical areas buy more of some items than others. If I know I will be near a sporting event, then I need more bottles of water. I serve a wide variety of customers in a wide variety of cultures and circumstances.

It's been said that in the world of comedy that the most important thing is....timing.

The ice cream truck has made a lot of people laugh. My spider hat has made a lot of people laugh. My spider hat has made a few babies cry.

Peeling onions makes people cry. I don't sell onions.

I sell ice cream novelties and more; I sell people a memory.

The entertainment and memory of the experience is why people enjoy a visit from an ice cream truck. A critical component which allows an encounter between the customer and me....is good timing. I've had several customers comment about the great timing. I've had many sales which would not have occurred one minute sooner or later.

As you read in the "Behavior Modification" chapter, timing affects behavior. The most dramatic example is probably the three women who ran to the street wearing nothing but a towel.

I love to arrive at games near the end, or at halftime. Track meets are good during the last third because many athletes have completed their events, but are still at the event.

It has taken me years to perfect my July 4th routine of timing. Based on where the different crowds gather and when they gather, I alter the timing of my arrival to gain the most sales opportunities.

During most of the season, there are over 60 different ice cream novelties in the truck I drive. That much variety confuses some people. By the end of the season, I have learned the preferences of my audience and tell Bob which items I need to have stocked.

The other key point I mentioned about leaving your audience wanting more is very important. People want what they can't have. When an ice cream truck shows up too often, most people begin to ignore it. My intense love of driving has benefitted my sales strategy of encountering thousands of potential customers a year. Most of those people do not see an ice cream truck too often.

Most sales opportunities would not exist at all if attempted at a different time. Even regular customers whom I see at somewhat varying times, are often not available if I alter my schedule too much or arrive on a different day of the week. There are many examples which involve crowds of people. Many fireworks crowds are great for sales, but they usually gather in places which at other times exhibit obvious signs of civilization.

However, certain time-specific crowds appear in places which are typically desolate.

There was a spot I encountered in July 2013 which I'm sure, at any other time of the year would produce almost zero sales if I sat there for hours and hours. The location is at an intersection of two roads outside a village in central Ohio with thousands of trees nearby and gently rolling terrain.

The timing that night was fantastic because that intersection is in a pocket of ideal geography for viewing the fireworks in the nearby village. I was stunned by how much ice cream I sold in a short time while barely moving the truck. I went to the village because of the fireworks show and found out that a special permit was needed to be there. I was lucky to leave town the way I did, so as to encounter the excellent location where people gathered to avoid the more intense chaos inside the village.

Another aspect of knowing my audience is utilizing the music options which exist in the truck I drive. The music box in most of the Toledo ice cream trucks have 32 songs to choose from. For over nine years, I had it set to play song #3 as I drove around. Song #3 is 44 seconds in length; it starts with a female voice saying, "HELLO ?". It then plays a pleasant melody for about 40 seconds with two seconds of silence, before repeating. Some people love the HELLO greeting; others hate it. One of my repeat customers who found it completely annoying told me to play a different song when arriving at his place. If he heard the "HELLO ?", he wasn't going to buy ice cream.

When I drive past horses or through a campground or near a park, I switch the music box to play song #2. It contains the sound of a galloping horse mixed in with the tune. Song #2 annoys me after ten minutes.

Song #7 is a short version of "Fur Elise" written by Beethoven. I choose that one when driving near a church or theater.

After briefly using alternate songs for certain locations, I switched back to song #3. Occasionally people would ask me how I can listen to it all day. I tell them that if they wouldn't be able to handle it, they shouldn't become an ice cream truck driver. I found it to be happy and pleasant. My niece was tired of it after hearing it for 8.5 hours when she rode with me one day.

I enjoyed the pleasantness of song #3 for over nine years, but then I was tired of it. In July 2013, I switched to song #16 which is a variation of "It's a Small World". Even though song #3 didn't bother me for nine years, I would occasionally briefly imagine hearing it, in November, after the end of my fifth through ninth seasons. My regular customer, Scott requested that I switch back to song #3 when I approach his house.

Another aspect of the music being played, is its volume. Of course, it's on maximum most of the time during the day. I reduce the volume during most night time city driving. My exact location within each city I drive at night has various levels of tolerance for ice cream music. If I'm deep within a campus area or downtown, I will have it at, or near maximum volume. In areas where it's best to use a much softer audio level, it still must be heard by the people on the street. I have received complaints from customers who couldn't hear it. The music creates Pavlov's Response.

During the day, I reduce the volume while driving past cemeteries or funeral homes. I also reduce the volume when approaching an Amish buggy because I don't know if the horse might be startled. When I approach athletic events, I briefly use maximum volume to get the attention of potential customers, but then turn it down.

I have learned:

Good timing is critical for successful sales.

Customer enjoyment and satisfaction is effected by having the right items available for them.

I learned more intensely that our society is spoiled.

Parties & Events

People frequently call Mister Frosty to arrange the presence of an ice cream truck at their event. Sometimes it's a birthday or graduation party. Those are nice because you show up and sell a lot of ice cream at one stop. When a company representative calls to have a truck for a company party, it's extra nice. Some companies have large budgets for such things and when the company is buying, most adults choose the items which primarily are more expensive. Sometimes I hire an assistant to help distribute the ice cream, depending on the nature of the event.

For my first big company event I talked to the father of Alex and Aaron, who were regular customers of mine. It was a two hour event. The company gave a ticket to each employee; there were about 200. The ticket was good for one item from the truck. Aaron collected tickets.

I marked down the price of each item upon giving it to Alex who handed the ice cream to the customer. We had a steady stream for over 70 minutes right after we arrived; then just small groups. I think the boys would have done it for free; they had a blast. I hired them the following year for the same event.

One of my favorite events was at a nursing home. On July 2nd, 2011 after I arrived at Mister Frosty, I began preparing the truck for the day. Brenda walked out of the office and asked if I could do an event "right NOW". It was 1:14 p.m. There was an event scheduled for 1:00, but no driver was there. Brenda told the customer and me, that the scheduled driver must have forgotten because of the chaos of the holiday coming up, and that she forgot to remind him. Brenda told the customer that she would send another driver immediately. There were a few other drivers in the lot at the time, but Brenda knew I was the best choice.

The customer called when there was no ice cream truck a little after 1:00, especially since the nursing home residents had been eagerly awaiting since 12:30. It might have been decades since some of them had gotten ice cream from a truck. Brenda put me on the telephone with one of the nurses to give me directions. Since the nursing home is located in metro Toledo, I knew EXACTLY the best way to get there FAST.

I got to the nursing home at 1:28

Three of the nurses immediately expressed to me their unhappiness about the arrival time of the truck. One of the nurses was very angry about the situation. After the patients and a few nurses, with the exception of the angry one, got their ice cream treats, I asked if they wanted to hear a poem about ice cream. When a few of them said, "Yes", I explained that I wrote it before I was an ice cream man and why it was written.

After I performed my poem "Ice Cream Dream", the angry nurse was smiling and started walking to the truck and I heard another nurse ask her, "Are you gonna get some ice cream now ?" She nodded.

After a few compliments about my poem, I asked if they wanted to hear one about spaghetti; they did.

After their compliments, I noted that if the other driver had gotten there on time, they wouldn't have heard my poetry. The formerly-angry nurse replied that my entertainment made up for the fact that they had to wait. She bought a second ice cream.

Brenda was relieved and Bob was happy that my poetry smoothed things over with the customer.

They called a few more times that year and specifically asked for the driver with the spider hat.

Here is my poem "Ice Cream Dream" which I wrote immediately after waking from the dream, which I had while employed as a driver for a small package delivery company. The truck in the dream was brown. This is the first poem of many which I have posted for free access on the world wide web.

I had a dream, about ice cream
I woke up smiling thinking about it
In my dream, I was at work
Things were hectic; I was going berserk

Then I drove past an ice cream shop
I needed a break, so I decided to stop
I parked the truck and went inside
I looked at the choices with eyes open wide
I got a triple scoop, on a cone
It tasted so awesome, I began to moan
It was rich, and velvety, and soft, and thick
It didn't seem cold, like it would melt very quick

It tasted so good, I thought the price would be big
So I reached into my pocket, and started to dig
I started pulling out money and I asked, "How much ?"
The girl looked at me and with a gentle touch
Said, "It's only a dollar; that's the price."
I was in **SHOCK**; it seemed too nice

Then I woke up, with no ice cream
But then I smiled, remembering my dream

One of my most important events never occurred; it was during my second season. A man was organizing a block party for his neighborhood. I typically drove through that neighborhood on Friday evenings my first few years of being an ice cream man. He wanted to pay based on the average price of the available items multiplied by the number of children at the party. If I had agreed to the man's terms, most of the children would have ordered the more expensive items. When I discussed the idea with Bob, he said, "That man is trying to get grocery store prices from a truck on his street." Bob pointed out that if the man wants those prices, then he can go to the grocery store and bring several boxes of popsicles and ice creams back to the party. If customers want the entertainment, the ice cream options, and the service provided by an ice cream truck, then they will have to pay more than what things cost at a grocery store. It was important for me to realize the value of the service provided by an ice cream truck, which goes far beyond the value of the items available from it.

Company parties scheduled by Brenda are great, but I prefer the events which are scheduled by me. Some of them are annually, during fireworks parties. Some are related to university activities. Sometimes random customers set them up with me.

One of the farthest events from Toledo I did was at a man's house who hosted his company party of about 20 people. It was in a town near Columbus. Since my sister lives near Columbus, I create routes between Toledo and Columbus which I drive a few times a year. When the man saw the truck, he assumed that I was from his area and returning for a party would be no big deal. After explaining my route strategy to the man, he asked how much it would cost to have the truck there. Based on my commission and fuel expenses, I told him that his company would need to buy at least $150 worth of ice cream from me. If I had been planning to be in his area for other purposes, I could have offered a better deal. I told him that there are ice cream trucks in Columbus. Almost everyone who has seen a Toledo ice cream truck, prefers it to other trucks. He wanted the truck I drive to be at his party; he agreed to the terms.

One of the man's co-workers paid me upon my arrival. They knew they were not going to want $150 worth of ice cream. Most of the people chose two items and the total was far less than $100. I was told that I received a big tip. I felt like I owed them more for their money. I asked them if they would like to hear my song about chocolate milk. They liked the idea. I added to the entertainment of their party by performing it. Many other customers have heard my chocolate milk song; it's my personal favorite of all the things I have written.

An artist who performs her own songs led to a special event. Crystal Bowersox is from my hometown area. During her association with the show "American Idol", she was in two parades in northwest Ohio. Several ice cream trucks were near the crowd during her Toledo parade. When she put on a concert at the Ottawa County fairgrounds near Oak Harbor, I was driving one of only two ice cream trucks in attendance.

My top sales day ever was because of an annual event. It was not a company party. It was not related to fireworks. Its participants were not expecting an ice cream truck. Due to rain in the area I was driving one day in 2011, I went farther from Toledo to find better skies. When I arrived in the area where the event was happening, many people asked why they didn't see me sooner. I learned about the event and planned to be there 52 weeks later.

The following year, I drove directly to the event site. I expected to have a great day. I had **no idea** that **by far**, it would be my best sales day ever.

Almost all of my previous best days were because of fireworks.

My previous #1 sales day was July 4th, 2008; I was in the truck 16 hours that day. I matched the sales total of July 4th, 2008 in about six hours on the day of my new event. Luckily, there was a point which a police officer asked me to move from where I was parked on the public street.

I typically wouldn't want to move from a prime selling spot, but I had been unprepared for the magnitude of sales. My beverages were SOLD OUT.

I was lucky that the freezer contained over 50 different items, because otherwise I would have missed many sales. I was able to drift away from the primary crowd, getting a break lasting more than 30 seconds.

I used my newly acquired smart phone to show a grocery store on a map. I bought the phone right before the 2012 season to be able to process credit card orders from customers. At the grocery store, I re-loaded on bottles of water and cans of Mountain Dew and Pepsi. I then went back to the crowd. I almost sold out of beverages again. Many of the ice cream novelties were also sold out.

I stocked heavy for the event in 2013, but the local police had changed the parameters for street vendors specifically for that event. It was still a great day. After I give up ice cream driving as a full-time commitment, I will want to lease a truck at least one day a year for that event.

My all-time favorite event was at Federal Express. I sold ice cream to its employees several times when they wanted to reward them for accident-free periods. I also was there for some other celebration which included a NASCAR race vehicle.

The reason FedEx was my favorite event, is because providing ice cream for the night shift in August 2007, allowed for my experimentation with selling ice cream at night to other members of the public. I elaborate on that in my chapter, "Night Driving".

I have learned:

Some people greatly appreciate the entertainment value of an ice cream truck.

Some companies have very large budgets which allow them to reward their employees in various ways.

Not all events are announced; being able to promptly respond to a sudden crowd greatly increases potential sales.

Are You Lost ?

During my third year in the truck, I extended my horizons a lot farther. I started driving through towns several counties from Toledo. I also learned that it was best to keep the music playing constantly. I previously would turn the music down, or off between towns. I realized though, that there are people everywhere who want ice cream from a truck.

The music is projected more than half a mile, so rural residents receive an indication that there is an ice cream truck coming, with time to react. The speed I drive is somewhat dictated by the distance between houses and the proximity of trees to the road. I have driven into hay fields and other off- road situations to serve the customer. I love when people don't make a big deal out of it.

There have been many times that I've been asked, "Are you lost ?". Or they ask where I'm going. Why does it matter where I'm going ? I drive from around to find people who want ice cream, that's where I'm going. It seems as if people expect an ice cream truck to be able to teleport from town to town without driving down the roads in between. Sometimes I give them a name of a nearby village where I am headed. Sometimes I have no idea what places are in front of me.

When I first began randomly exploring without a map, I took advantage of northwest Ohio's flat terrain. I would look for a water tower, or set of grain elevators in the distance. I finally bought an Ohio map book which shows every road. The map shows tiny communities which sometimes have fewer than 50 people. Those communities are great because they force me to drive a little slower. The slightest interest in an ice cream truck is quickly shown in areas like that.

My natural love of exploring works well in an ice cream truck. My desire to see a new place sometimes creates a reward for me and a new customer. Usually when I drive far off the beaten path, my fuel expense climbs beyond the return from sales. Sometimes I am rewarded by a great photo opportunity.

About once a year, I am rewarded by seeing the pure joy on the face of a child who is able to buy something from an ice cream truck. That child who lives in the middle of nowhere and never even thought of having the possibility for that occurrence, beams with happiness.

There are times when other circumstances cause me to drive outside the normal patterns. If there are friends or family I am trying to visit, I will go places which might otherwise never experience an ice cream truck.

My friend Joy informed me that she lives on a dead-end road outside the city and her two daughters would like a visit from an ice cream truck. She lives much closer to Chicago than Toledo and learned on-line that I was near Chicago. When I was on the way to Joy's home, a few other kids on the dead-end road got excited when they saw an ice cream truck drive by. They figured that I would return in a few minutes. I had lunch with Joy's family, so it took a little longer. The children's mom told them that I had to come back that way at some point in time.

I had one other situation where people on a dead-end road thought I would be right back. My friends Sherry and Jim live at the end of the road and invited me to stay for dinner, so it was an hour until I returned to the eager customers.

Because of my explorations, there are times when I actually am lost. I have gained many customers by stopping to look at my map. When people see me stopped for any reason, they are more likely to run for ice cream. Some of the rural areas, where ice cream truck visits are extremely rare, have created my favorite stops.

My all-time favorite stop occurred on a Sunday evening in May. I left a town of 200 people which I used to visit about every three weeks. I headed north on the state route to the next town. It was almost 8:30.

The sun was ten minutes away from touching the horizon. It was 53 degrees Fahrenheit. I put the cruise control on 55 MPH. As I was driving along, with zero traffic on the road with houses more than a quarter mile from each other, I noticed something unusual in my side mirror.

My initial thought was, that there were small radio-controlled toy cars catching up with me. I glanced back again to realize that there were two young men on off-road all-terrain vehicles chasing me. A man on a dirt bike was with them. I tapped the brake to release the cruise control and slowed to 40 MPH. They were soon near my rear bumper, but made no indication that they wanted me to stop. I then thought that maybe they weren't chasing me, so I began accelerating. At that moment, the man on the motorcycle sped up to catch me and when he was beside my driver's door, he mimed licking an ice cream cone. I then knew they definitely wanted ice cream, so I pulled over.

Their faces were very cold from chasing me in the cool evening. They told me that they were in the woods and heard the ice cream music. They had no particular ice cream choice in mind, so I told them that while they were deciding upon their choices, I wanted to create a photograph.

The reasons that it is my favorite stop, is the scene of them chasing me.

I also love the way that he indicated that he wanted me to stop. I love that it was only 53 degrees. I love that I was going 55 MPH. I love that I captured the scene with my camera. I very much love that three people did whatever they could, to chase me and catch me. They vividly proved that my method of ice cream truck driving is appreciated.

My second-favorite stop also involved a chase. It involved more people doing whatever it takes to get their ice cream from a truck.

It was late afternoon in early June, on a road I only drive on about twice a year. It's between Columbus and Athens. The road is curvy with no houses for miles. It's the only road between two different areas I cruise. The scenery is beautiful with a stream along one side of the road and rocky cliffs along the other side. As I went past a few houses before reaching the section of road absent of housing, a family heard the ice cream music. They quickly jumped into their Jeep Wrangler and chased me for a couple of miles on the winding road. They were very excited to catch me.

My many route adventures started to be known among the other ice cream drivers in Toledo. My successful sales figures were somewhat known among other drivers at Mister Frosty. Since my sales numbers didn't drop as much as theirs halfway through the season, they naturally want to know where I drive. I too easily share information about myself; I try to not have secrets. Bob would have to repeatedly remind me to keep my mouth shut. A few of the drivers would joke around about the fact that they were going to follow me to find out where I go. I would tell them that even the C.I.A. couldn't follow me without my knowledge. I drive in many obscure areas and frequently encounter zero traffic. As my routes began to get farther from Toledo, I would tell other drivers exactly where I was going; I knew they weren't going to go there.

Occasionally my presence in far away places was reported back to Mister Frosty because some people know what a Toledo ice cream truck looks like compared to others in that area. I found out during my road trip to Minnesota that my presence was being broadcast on social media.

I have many regular customers in central Ohio because of the routes I have developed while exploring. The Columbus ice cream trucks do not travel very far from the city. One of my regular customers who lives outside a small village southeast of Columbus, told me that her son had seen an ice cream truck in a movie. He asked her if they exist in reality. She told him, "They do exist in real life, just not around here." I showed up on their road less than one year later.

Due to the fact that I drive over 1,000 miles every week of the season, I must maintain a speed in the truck which combines time efficiency with possibly finding new customers. Many customers have demonstrated that their desire is strong enough to do whatever it takes to cause me to stop. It would be nice to be able to give everyone more time to react to the presence of the truck, but some people are annoyed by the ice cream music. I drive fast in some places to reduce the annoyance factor for those not wanting ice cream.

I feel bad that there have been people who were not able to react fast enough to my presence, to notify me to stop. Since I don't work for the Red Cross, I have not viewed my presence as a necessity. If the ice cream truck were providing emergency services, my driving strategy would be different. There have been a few occasions in which the truck did provide medical aid. In those instances, I did not charge the citizens for the bottle of water that they NEEDED.

Two of those incidents involved people who had gotten maced. They both happened while I was parked downtown at night. Both of the victims were women. The second one had been too close to another person who was pepper-sprayed by police.

Other free bottles of water which I have distributed, were to people who had cuts. I also have given away my extra cardboard boxes which have been used for various purposes.

The Prom

The best result for everyone involved, of someone possibly thinking I was lost, occurred on my way to Bowling Green one night. It was a Friday in April shortly after 10 p.m. I had plenty of time to be in Bowling Green. As I wandered on rural roads, I encountered County Road 16. I drove many miles on 16 before someone came out to the road as I approached. Several high school seniors were gathered and were curious about the appearance of an ice cream truck. I explained where I was going and why I chose road 16. After chatting with the guys a while, Ben suggested that I take them to their Prom in the ice cream truck the following week. Several friends have ridden in the truck at different times, but this was different. I thought he was kidding. Ben said it would be great to ride around his town selling ice cream and then be dropped off at the Prom. When I realized that he was serious, we exchanged contact info.

My schedule was open the following Saturday and I thought it would be a fun situation. Ben had me meet them in the parking lot of a local store. Parents and siblings were there with cameras and several people bought ice cream before we began the trip to Prom. One of the boys said our first stop needed to be where his parents were so that they could get pictures of the kids. I received a tip there of freshly fried frog legs and other food they were selling for their fundraiser. Dan brought his girlfriend; she was the only girl in the group. The group enjoyed selling ice cream and have a fun memory that they will probably discuss at high school reunions.

"Remember when we rode to Prom ? in the ice cream truck with Pineapple 16"

The following year, Dan's girlfriend Abbey was then a senior. She went to high school in a neighboring town. Of course she told many friends about her ride to the Prom the previous year. She wanted to do it again.

I picked up the kids at a park in their town where they had been getting photos with their parents. We rode around town selling ice cream to their friends. It was great to have them direct me to customers so I didn't have to wander aimlessly around their village.

The awesome part was when I dropped them off at their school. Their school sets up bleachers near the entrance to Prom for spectators of their red carpet introductions. The Prom attendees had cards to fill out with the names they wanted to be introduced as. When we arrived, my riders bought face popsicles from me to eat as they were walking in. The guys added the name of their popsicle to their name.

An example of other Prom attendees arrival is this: "Next we have Suzy M and Tommy B arriving in a car driven by Suzy's dad"

When my riders were announced, it was like this: "Next we have Jacob Ninja Turtle N, Micah Bugs Bunny M...arriving in the ice cream truck driven by Pineapple 16"

Driving in the parade of vehicles was fun. I found out later that one of the kids arrived in a FedEx truck driven by his uncle. I believe my passengers got more fun attention because of their ride. I wouldn't have thought of that situation myself.

A few weeks before the Prom, while I was in another neighboring town. A kid said to me, "You're taking me to Prom in this truck." I figured that he must be a friend of Abbey, but he seemed much younger than a senior. I asked him if he was Abbey's friend. He didn't know Abbey. He didn't know anyone from Abbey's village. He knew nothing about my Prom plans. He was a 7th-grader planning for the future, thinking that the ice cream truck would be the best way to arrive at his Prom.

I learned that:

The farther I travel from Toledo, the better my sales become.

People who live farther away from impulsive purchasing opportunities are more likely to buy cans of soda from me.

It is always good to keep exploring new roads, and new communities.

An ice cream truck can serve the public in ways which go beyond entertainment and fun.

Amish Paradise

My third year in the truck involved my service horizons stretching farther from Toledo. I began exploring an area with some Amish residents. I would occasionally see Amish people waving at me as I drove by, and didn't think that they were trying to get me to stop. Since people wave at me ALL the time, I'm used to primarily ignoring that gesture as a signal to stop and treating it only as a greeting. One day however, as I drove past an Amish house the dad waved at me in a way which seemed to suggest he might want ice cream. I was probably only going 35 to 40 MPH past his house, so I hit the brakes, turned around and went back to investigate. His children began gathering in the barnyard near my truck with looks of excitement combined with curiosity and astonishment. We greeted each other and he asked what I had. After pointing out the menu of about 60 ice cream novelties, he chose some treats for his family.

After I left and continued on my way down the road, I immediately used my cellular telephone to call two friends to share my excitement. I did not know at the time that I would establish business relationships with dozens of Amish families.

My dad and grandpa had a farming business together when I was a child, so I spent a lot of time around the farming environment. Since most ice cream truck drivers are from the city, I am probably the only ice cream man whose dad and grandpa had a dairy farm. My friend Howard is also a farmer, so I still get to experience the farm atmosphere, which is far different than city life where I have resided most of my adult life.

It was VERY exciting for me to experience the tiniest hint of the Amish environment because their entire culture is so different from what I am used to.

My fourth year involved a little more time near that Amish area. I had a few more Amish customers, but nothing stood out and I didn't specifically go down their roads very much. I usually slow down when encountering houses where I've previously sold ice cream, but that still leaves VERY little time for people to react to the presence of an ice cream truck near their home. Many of the Amish farms are back long lanes giving them even shorter time to react.

In October 2008, my friend Howard was shopping for farm equipment in the area where my Amish customers live. I chauffeured him in his car to the farm he needed to go to, since I love driving and knew the area. After the farm negotiations, I asked the farmer if he ever heard an ice cream truck going down his road. He smiled and said, "Yeah, I have."

I informed him that I was the one driving the truck. He advised me that I should slow down near the Amish houses because there is a very good chance that they would buy from me. The next summer, I did.

I soon learned that many Amish families wanted to buy ice cream from me. Since they don't have electricity, they can't store it like those of us with refrigerators and freezers in our homes can. They occasionally ride their buggies to town several miles away to get ice cream, but need to eat it right away. The novelty and convenience of having an ice cream truck on their farm is too much to resist. Since many of the Amish families consist of six to fourteen children, most of them want gallons of ice cream. Buying MANY individual ice cream novelties is very expensive.

I discovered that the best way to serve my Amish customers is to buy a few gallons and half-gallons of ice cream from a store in Toledo on the days when I do my Amish route. The price I charge them is the same that they would pay in their local small town store. I end up receiving about the same amount of commission. The half-gallon ice cream containers come in a variety of flavors, however one Amish man said to me, "We don't like fancy." Some of the families prefer peanut butter ice cream, or cookies and cream, or fudge marble, but I mostly sell vanilla. Some of them also buy a few of the regular novelties available from the ice cream truck freezer. A few of them also like a can of cold Mountain Dew.

I typically turn down the music after stopping to sell ice cream. Many of my Amish customers have told me to turn it up. They rarely hear music of any kind, so they very much enjoy hearing it. Many of them have danced while near the truck. Some of the families have requested that I return to see if they might want ice cream the next time I'm in the neighborhood. Some of them have also told me to stop at the next farm because they know that the family there would like ice cream; it is often their relative.

Just like with non-Amish customers, I learn which customers prefer what items and how frequently they would like me to be there. Another aspect of having repeat customers is getting to know each other on a little bit more of a personal level. Some of my Amish customers enjoy seeing photographs of mine which are on my iPad. Some of them also enjoy hearing songs on my iPod instead of the ice cream music.

Two of the Amish families have my telephone number. I have the number of their English neighbors. If I know I'm going to visit a couple of days ahead of time, I can order pies or cinnamon rolls.

One summer after several weeks of not doing my Amish route, Dan called me to ask when I was going to be there. It's always helpful to maintain good communication.

A major selling strategy which I have implemented during hot weather is driving my Amish route. Most Americans are addicted to air conditioning and sales go way down when the temperature is above 83 degrees Fahrenheit (28 degrees Celsius).

Since Amish don't have air conditioning, they especially enjoy my arrival. It is also more convenient for them on those days. It is far more difficult for them to enjoy ice cream at home when it's hot because it takes too long to get home from the store with newly purchased ice cream.

At least one of the families keeps ice cream cones in stock at their house. When I show up with a five-quart bucket of ice cream, they are very happy.

Most of the times that I do my Amish route, I also encounter English customers at various points between it and Toledo. There was one day, however, which was 100% Amish; it was a great day. I had good sales and I had pleasant interactions with my customers and the environment.

I learned that:

I need to drive much slower when driving in an Amish community.

I need to have different items on the truck to satisfy the desires of Amish customers.

Other than ice cream music, most of the Amish people I see, hear no music at all.

Hand signals which many people use to signal that they don't want ice cream, means the opposite from many Amish people.

Many Amish families expect me to stop at their house even if they don't want ice cream.

Night Driving

As my route horizons expanded, my available selling hours challenged my logistical abilities. I usually would try to work my routes so that they were a big loop with my distance from Mister Frosty becoming less as the day was waning. However on certain days, especially Saturdays, I would be selling ice cream in an area very far from home with a slow return rate back to Toledo. The sun would set and I knew Bob would wonder what happened to me if I got back too late. I would choose a direct route back to the city, but I would leave the ice cream music playing and the display lights on.

As I drove along at 55 MPH, some people would still be outside and become aware of my presence on their road. If they wanted ice cream, they had a few seconds to run to the road, or flash their porch lights, or figure out some way to signal me that they wanted me to stop. Ice cream desire causes people to get creative when they see an ice cream truck zooming past their location.

Sometimes a group of people would be having a bonfire, or party, or it was just the case that they didn't ever see an ice cream truck any other time and wanted to take advantage of the circumstance. I soon learned that there were plenty of people interested in buying ice cream from a truck after dusk. I soon became the last driver to return almost every night that I drove.

My ability to truly be a night time ice cream man, came in August 2007. Many thanks go to Federal Express for having the ice cream truck deliver ice cream to its employees as a reward for having zero injuries during their August focus on working safely. The local FedEx hub has three different shifts for its part-time employees, and they wanted the truck more than just the typical twilight time. I was there for forty minutes to cover their break period, then could sell ice cream on the street before returning to FedEx for the next shift's break period.

The key factor is that the night shift required that I be there at mid-night. Bob didn't want to wait for me to return at that time of night, so he gave me a key to the gate; I could then return the truck to Mister Frosty when I was done at FedEx.

Even though it was only one mile back to Mister Frosty, I drove to the campus area near the University of Toledo. I knew that the college crowd would still be partying until after 2 a.m. so I wasn't done for the day yet. Sales were good and many UT students were excited to see an ice cream truck driving around so late. I did not know how much success I would have with night sales at that point, but knew that continuing to explore that realm of sales opportunities was a good idea.

The timing was excellent to start night driving because sales always go down in late summer. With the college school year about to start, I knew where to find hundreds of potential customers. The rest of that season, I was very busy on Thursday, Friday and Saturday nights until 3 a.m.

I learned that along with driving in the neighborhoods filled with college students, a good place to briefly park late at night was in front of saloons. It wasn't just the college students who were excited to see me. Some of the saloons have regular customers whose average age is higher than 40. When people leave their house to go out on the town, to spend money, to have fun, they enjoy extra pleasures which might randomly occur.

Spending a few dollars for an ice cream novelty from a truck, brings many people a bit of happiness far beyond what they could generally receive any other way. Many people wanted photographs with me and photographs of the truck.

Some of the saloons specifically enjoyed my arrival and would announce to their customers when I showed up. For me, it was nice to sit in one place for a change. Depending on the public interest, I would stay at one place anywhere from five to forty minutes. Another variable was how many other places I could possibly expect reactions from. Over time I have learned which places want ice cream at which times. Some places are best before midnight; others are better between midnight and 2:00.

Sometimes I've been busy selling ice cream until almost 4:00 a.m. I have sold beyond that time too.

Some late night customers told me that they didn't even want ice cream; they were only buying it from me because I was there at such a late hour.

The summer of 2008 involved consistently selling ice cream late at night Wednesday through Saturday. Wednesdays were Goth night at a saloon in Bowling Green. Bigger night sales occurred in September after the universities were back in session.

Selling ice cream at night allows me to experience a greater diversity among the citizens I encounter. It also highlights judgements of people who randomly see an ice cream truck at night.

Village Idiot

My friend Kelly rode with me one night to experience night sales in downtown Toledo. Toledo's sales were slow, so Kelly suggested that we try the crowd at the Village Idiot in Maumee. They have live music every night and draw a good crowd of people who enjoy ice cream truck visits.

The Village Idiot Saloon has become my number one saloon to visit while in the truck at night.

Terri is the girl who collects the cover charge at the door of the Village Idiot. On Terri's birthday, Sully, who also works there, had me take Terri and Nikki for a ride around the neighborhood. It was 11 p.m. on a Sunday. It was supposed to only take five minutes. It's also good to let potential customers at the bar realize that I'm not going to sit there all night. A short trip for a few blocks promotes awareness of that fact. We drove a few blocks from the bar and stopped at one of their friend's houses. A man came out to the truck carrying a guitar. He put his guitar on the freezer and then rode with us. As we were headed back to the Village Idiot, I encountered a four-way stop at an intersection next to the Maumee police department. Here's where night-specific judgement comes in.

While we were stopped at guitar-man's house, one of his neighbors called the police to report that someone was selling drugs from an ice cream truck on her street.

Right after an officer became aware of that call, she walked out to her cruiser and saw that an ice cream truck was driving past the police department. As I left the intersection, I noticed the police car aggressively approaching my location. I wondered if the officer perceived my stop as a violation. I was pulled over by the police car right in front of the house where one of the regulars of the Village Idiot resides. I later learned that Dan was watching the television show, "COPS", when suddenly red and blue lights were dancing around in the darkness on his street and through his windows.

Of course, I was wearing my spider hat. My three passengers were a bit giddy from the circumstances. The officer approached the serving window and exchanged bits of recognition with my passengers. She then asked if I had been drinking. I don't drink, and Terri pointed that out to the officer. My happy demeanor and other aspects of the situation caused the officer to conduct a sobriety test anyway. It was my first one ever. It was quite interesting to be doing it with my spider hat on, next to the ice cream truck, on a Sunday night in Maumee.

The officer told us about the telephone call.

Another perception which I have become aware of, is that many people believe drugs might be available when they see me at night. I've had people ask me for things I've never heard of before. I've had people ask for things "not listed on the menu". When people ask if I have drugs, I reply, "only caffeine". Depending on how long they remain standing there, I will add to my response, "monosodium glutamate", because it's in the potato chips. One of my friends who was attending the university informed me that some people think I'm an undercover police officer.

I love observing the reactions of people when they first encounter the truck at night. Most of the people are college students. Many of them haven't had an ice cream truck for many years. I occasionally am able to hear discussions between people discussing whether or not it's odd to see an ice cream truck at midnight.

I love it when one person tells another that it's no big deal. I love it when I hear someone tell another, as I drive by at night, "Only in... (insert location)". They are probably correct that there isn't another ice cream truck driving around at night. However, they don't know that I drive in several cities at night.

For me, it's also very different to be in the city. During the day, I only want to drive in towns too small to have a stoplight. At night, everything changes. Chicago is a perfect example. It would be impossible to sell ice cream during the day in downtown Chicago. There is too much traffic, too much chaos. At night, it's easier to find a spot to pull over.

At night, people on the street are ready to spend money.

Another place I enjoy driving at night is near campgrounds. Campers are doing things during the day, but after dusk, an ice cream truck provides something they are very unlikely to possess.

Most of my night driving involves far less financial rewards per hour than day driving. My paternal grandpa told me more than once, "You're spending your time one of two ways: you're either making money, or you're spending money."

As a single man, if I weren't driving the truck around making money, I would be somewhere else spending money. When I had a girlfriend, my night driving didn't occur as much. Once in a while, sales are awesome at night.

One of my top ten sales days ever, involved almost half my sales occurring after 10:30 p.m.

Another advantage of driving at night is when bad weather exists. I've had sales days start after dusk because of bad weather. Rain keeps many people inside during the day, but at night, the bar crowd is still out wandering around. At night, they don't care if it's only 32 degrees, they still buy ice cream.

The most common (and possibly only) occurrence for night driving which other drivers experience is during fireworks shows.

I learned:

When people are out at night in the city to spend money at the bar, they will also spend money on ice cream.

People in rural areas who have bonfires and other parties late at night, also enjoy a visit from an ice cream truck.

Night driving makes inclement weather less relevant.

The novelty of night driving causes people who don't even want ice cream to buy it anyway.

FIREWORKS !!

The best place to drive an ice cream truck is near a crowd waiting to watch fireworks. They are out of the house, lined up and ready for excitement. Depending on exactly where the fireworks display is, many of the people do not usually purchase ice cream from a truck. The special occasion of a fireworks show, gives many people the added desire for ice cream from a truck. Evenings are typically best for ice cream sales and a fireworks show accentuates that. I have learned during some of my recurring fireworks shows to not worry so much about big sales prior to 6:00. Depending on where the fireworks are, I plan recreational activities for the early part of the day. There is always a sales crescendo until the fireworks display starts.

During my first season in the truck, Bob suggested to me, driving 80 minutes from Toledo for a fireworks show, near the village of Kalida. It was on July 11th, so I had no other fireworks options. I returned to that site every year after that, until it no longer displayed fireworks. I gained several new customers during that first visit, who I ended up seeing once a year for seven years. I add that area to my route a few times a year now.

There is still one fireworks location I have done every year, and it's on July 4th. I have various regular customers on that day which I have seen only on July 4th. There is a family farm half a mile outside the city where I have been going every year since 2004. They have a huge party with many grandchildren, cousins, et cetera. Per their request, I arrive about 7:30. After I sell ice cream to the family, I am told to grab a plate and get some dinner from their potluck feast in the barn. My friend's daughter, Maria also joined in the feast when she rode with me. I hired Maria a few times to help me on July 4th because it is always my busiest evening. Most of my best sales days are because of fireworks, and most of those, are July 4th.

The last few years, my average number of fireworks shows is sixteen. Depending on the year, the first week of July has a fireworks show every day. Various other festivals add a fireworks display in June or late July, or August. After a couple of years of driving, I realized the financial benefit of finding a fireworks show.

Even if the show were hours from Toledo, it was usually a financial gain to go there. I always enjoy the drive and exploration of new territory. A few of my experiments didn't work and I'm better at identifying unfavorable scenarios upon arriving at a new location. I still have to drive there though to find out.

I VERY much enjoy giving new people in desolate areas the opportunity to buy ice cream from a truck.

More than one of the unfavorable fireworks events I have explored, is due to the fact that there is a huge festival associated with it. Huge festivals create too many traffic restrictions for me. If the crowd is inaccessible, I'm not going to sell very much. I have suddenly traveled to another fireworks site after discovering the bad situation on at least two occasions.

I also have altered my fireworks plans due to bad weather. One of them took me much farther from Toledo, but it paid off. I also again enjoyed the satisfaction of giving new people the ice cream truck opportunity.

I enjoy the Sylvania fireworks because after the big show, I drive through one of the neighborhoods at the edge of the city where many families start setting off their own displays. It's the only time I can drive through that type of residential area at night with the ice cream music at full volume. It seems like a war zone with sparks and bottle rockets streaking through the sky in every direction. Children are running around screaming in the chaos. I always wonder when they get to bed after all the excitement and high-fructose corn syrup.

My July 4th fireworks location is not near Toledo. I enjoy using the county roads to return to Toledo, searching for private fireworks displays as I drive. When I see fireworks, I think of them as a flare which signals, **"Hey, we're having a party and we want ice cream from a truck."**

I love it when I have a little time to enjoy the show myself. Depending on where the show is, customers lose interest in ice cream as soon as the show starts, or keep me busy during the entire display.

My first fireworks road trip was in 2008. The location (G.H.) is 220 miles from Toledo. I knew that if I was selling ice cream until after dusk, it would be better to spend the night in that area and return home the next day. I elaborate on that in the "Road Trippin" chapter.

The success of that fireworks road trip has caused me to repeat it every year. There are a few customers in G.H. whom I see every year.

They know that before the fireworks, I will show up for my annual visit. Other fireworks shows have caused me to build road trips around them.

A key fact which I learned my first year, is that, if a fireworks display is in a small town or any rural environment, many spectators will stay home or gather places other than the immediate display area.

A key strategy for finding many potential customers at an event, is to drive around. During the several years I have driven an ice cream truck, I have noticed that almost all the other drivers tend to park during events. When fireworks are shot from a high school, or another venue, other ice cream truck drivers will arrive early, usually by 6:00. Many fireworks shows in June or July start at 10:00. Four hours of sitting in one location only serves the population who are intrigued enough to walk to wherever the truck is parked. I don't like to treat the truck like a building. I use the wheels to drive around the area of the school and other neighborhoods within good visual range of the display.

During the summer of 2010, I went to many fireworks shows; several of them were my first time. I love the excitement of possibly discovering a crowd which doesn't normally see ice cream trucks. One of my new ones that summer was in a large city where not only do the people see trucks a lot, but they saw trucks a lot that night.

Upon my arrival near the event, I immediately spotted several other ice cream trucks. At first, I was a bit overwhelmed. I'm used to going places where I am driving the only one. Occasionally, there is ONE other truck. Since there were so many, I wasn't worried about infringing upon another driver's turf. I drove around the area scouting the scene to learn the parking pattern of the crowd. It was a large shopping area, so there were numerous parking lots with the crowd scattered. In that situation, I could see the benefit for most of the drivers to sit in one spot. I saw nine other ice cream trucks at the event that night. Sometimes there were people with two different trucks within 100 yards.

I slowly drove through the lots and made some sales. One woman said to me, "I was wondering when a truck was gonna come by." She could have walked a short distance to another truck, but she followed my philosophy that a store with wheels should come to you.

Another benefit of exploring new fireworks locations, is the route along the way to the fireworks. Some of my repeat customers are 52 weeks after the first encounter. One of my annual customers is Mike. Mike hosts his own fireworks show and party at his rural residence the Saturday before July 4th. I randomly drove past his house one year on the day of the party. I was informed that the crowd would be much bigger that night. I usually arrive about 11 p.m. and am there for an hour. I am always invited to join the party, which I do after selling ice cream to the crowd. Several party-goers at Mike's are aware that I perform songs I've written, so I get requests.

While selling ice cream at fireworks shows, **I have learned:**

Many members of the crowd live on roads which are not visited by an ice cream truck. Those people are extremely excited about the opportunity to enjoy ice cream novelties.

Other vendors who sell glow bracelets enjoy the presence of an ice cream truck because of the large illuminated vehicle drawing attention from people's isolated group. Some vendors typically buy a beverage from me. Some like to be near the truck for more sales of their own.

Fireworks shows create parties in a large area around the display area. As long as they are within visual range, the party can be several miles away. Driving around is essential to serve the most people.

Many communities have fireworks displays during festivals which have no connection to Independence Day.

Road Trippin'

The title of this chapter has a double meaning. This chapter is about road trips which involve not returning to Toledo at the end of the day. Some of the road trips were adventurous and fun beyond typical expectations of what I associate with time spent making money. I am not familiar from first-hand experience with the high caused by drugs, but I've experienced many highs from traveling to new places far from Toledo, to find people wanting ice cream from a truck. Many of the road trips I created are as much about fun and adventure, as they are about making money.

I often find it difficult to believe that my actions are not entirely selfish.

In May 2008, while deciding plans for my trip to Cincinnati to run the Flying Pig Marathon, I told Bob that I would not be driving the truck that weekend, unless he let me keep it over night in Cincinnati. He could have put another driver in the truck, but I had proven to be better with sales than his other drivers. He thought about my proposition for about one second and then replied, "Take the truck." For me the fuel expense for my first ice cream road trip was irrelevant because I was going to Cincinnati anyway. It became a great opportunity to explore new counties and find new people who don't usually have an ice cream truck visit. I had already driven my personal car in all 88 Ohio counties during previous map-collection adventures, but this was my first time driving the ice cream truck anywhere near Dayton or Cincinnati.

I sold ice cream in a few towns on the way to Cincinnati. It was rainy that day, so I only explored VERY small towns near the interstate. My primary mission was getting to the marathon expo to pick up my T-shirt and race packet. I had a serious foot injury three days before that, and doubted my ability to run, but had already registered and was hoping my foot would be strong enough by Sunday morning.

After the expo, I explored areas near the city and then when it was dark, explored the campus area near University of Cincinnati. I typically only sleep two and a half hours the night before a marathon, so I didn't worry about my lack of sleep from selling ice cream so late. I still had trouble walking Sunday morning, so running 26 miles was not a good idea. I slept a little more after realizing that I wasn't racing that day. I watched some of the early finishers and began my trek back to Toledo. It took all day to get there, because I went through every little town I could along the way, to give new people the opportunity to buy ice cream from a truck.

One of my college roommates, Eric, lives in Greenville, so I went there to sell ice cream. Greenville is much larger than my ideal town-size preference. I primarily just wanted to see Eric. I kept working my way back to Toledo, stopping in as many small towns along the way, that I could serve, before dusk.

I was disappointed about not being able to compete in the marathon, but the success of that trip made me realize that traveling in the truck was a good idea.

Fireworks Road Trip

When one of my regular customers told me about a fireworks show which occurs the first weekend of August, I was initially skeptical about its financial success. The location is over 200 miles from Toledo, but I figured that I should try it. Just like when I went to Cincinnati for the marathon, it was a two-day road trip.

The journey to my target was great in allowing me to explore new towns and see new people. The fireworks crowd was enormous and the fireworks display was very good. The return on Sunday was phenomenal. At the very beginning of my day, I drove down a road leading to a small town and was stopped by a man and his daughter. They were surprised to see an ice cream truck on their road. After I explained why I was there, the dad told me that if I am ever in the area again, I should be sure to stop at their house. I returned 52 weeks later. After a couple of years, I learned that he marked it on the calendar and told his daughter a few days in advance that the ice cream truck is coming on Sunday. 2013 marked my sixth visit to that family.

As I continued my trek back to Toledo, I encountered many towns which had not seen an ice cream truck for 30 years. Several people told me that they specifically remember that is was 30 years. One of the villages is named Perrinton. The residents there embraced my presence more than anywhere else I had been, which is a lot. I was busy for over an hour.

Several residents bought ice cream from me a second time after they learned that it would be a year until my return. Several of them asked and I replied, "If I return, it will be in 52 weeks." One of the residents created some photographs of me with her grandchildren; we have repeated that tradition every year since.

Another Perrinton resident asked for more details about my potential return the following year. She told me that she was on a committee which had discussed possible plans for a summer festival in their town. When I returned 52 weeks later, she mentioned it again. When the village organized their summer festival, it turned out to be the same weekend that I had been showing up. Most festivals and many villages want money from ice cream trucks just for being there. The residents and officials of Perrinton appreciate my presence and the service I provide in their village and do not ask for any financial benefit.

During the last two summers, I added Perrinton to my Saturday route on the way to the annual fireworks show. I let the residents know that I will return the following day. On Sunday, I tell them that it will be another year until they see me again.

By the end of the day that first year, with the sun long gone, I was still very far from Toledo. My plan worked. I was able to sell lots of ice cream on the way to Toledo and expose new crowds to the joy of ice cream truck visits. The third year, I decided to stay in that area Sunday night, with my return to Toledo on Monday involving more sales.

Another house that I stopped at during the third year, in a different town, did not immediately have people exiting to buy ice cream. It appeared as if someone was home, so I exited the truck and went to their front door. They seemed surprised to see me and I didn't recognize them. I asked if they had moved in there, in the last twelve months. They had. I told them that the previous owner bought ice cream when I went down that road once a year, so that's why I stopped.

They decided to continue the tradition.

The sales numbers for the fireworks day were not as good after the first year, partly due to the weather. The Sunday numbers were always strong, partly due to my entire day devoted to driving. If one town was weak with sales, that gave me more time to spend in another place. My memory allows me to keep track of which places are good or bad for future visits to an area.

When I started creating road trips to unknown areas, it was because of fireworks. Another incentive for traveling occurs in late summer due to the fact that sales go way down in the areas served early in the season. My net income for road trips is typically non- existent due to the large amount of diesel fuel I must buy. I am rewarded in other ways. My intense love of driving and desire to explore is satisfied. I also encounter different photo opportunities.

In September 2008, I drove the truck to Athens, Ohio for the first time. It was a Wednesday and I drove the most one-day ice cream truck miles of my career. I drove 464 miles from Toledo to Athens.

Pennsylvania and West Virginia were part of that day. I didn't sell any ice cream in Pennsylvania because I didn't find a road which I could drive slow enough on. The roads are curvy and I do not like to create a traffic hazard by impeding traffic. I was in PA for one hour. I had a couple of stops in WV before dusk when I returned to Ohio and sold ice cream in downtown Marietta. After serving a couple of customers in Marietta, I was ready to try Athens. Athens is home to Ohio University which has many students with a great desire for ice cream truck opportunities.

Since I showed up on a Wednesday, I didn't fully realize the sales potential of visiting that location. It would be a year and a half until I learned how amazing Athens and OU are for ice cream visits.

During 2009, I only went to the Columbus area twice, other than for a fireworks show. My sister lives near Columbus, so I could work a route on the way down and spend the night at my sister's. I would return the next day and drive through other new towns or neighborhoods. Since some of my typical routes in northwest Ohio involve starting and finishing in Toledo with 180 miles driven, it makes sense to me to add a few dozen miles to my daily total for a completely new experience.

In **August 2010**, I found out about a fireworks show in a small town more than 270 miles from Toledo, in northern Michigan. If you use your hand to represent Michigan, Hillman is near the top joint of your index finger. By that time, Bob was used to me stretching the perceptions of how an ice cream truck should be operated. For me, it was a great exploration, and time away from my typical routine. I loaded the freezer extra-heavy. Preparing for a fireworks show requires extra inventory of certain items. My first big road trip added even more.

I left Toledo on a Friday and drove a few hours on the highway before hitting small roads in an attempt to find customers. I had a good day.

My sales dollars slightly exceeded my miles driven. When my commission exceeds the amount I spent on fuel, I love that day. I also love it when I can introduce an ice cream truck to new people.

On Saturday, I kept going north toward the village where the fireworks would be that night. Northern Michigan has A LOT of trees. There were places where I was sure that no houses existed within five miles in any direction from where I was. I left the music playing though, as I drove down the road. One of my favorite stops occurred when a man on an off-road four-wheeler waved me down. He was with friends riding trails in the forest. He heard the ice cream music getting louder as he happened to be near the road. He was in disbelief until he saw the truck.

Considering the high percentage of miles I had traveled towards the Mackinac Bridge, it made sense to me to go all the way there to get some great photographs. After the fireworks Saturday night, I drove to Mackinaw City before sunrise. I had no interest in trying to sell ice cream early Sunday morning, so after my very long photo session, I started back to Toledo. When it was later in the morning, I began to drive back to Toledo through small towns in search of customers.

As I mentioned in the "Behavior Modification" chapter, many people in various locations gave me a thumbs-up or created a cheering gesture. I was in areas that haven't seen an ice cream truck for decades. Some of them never had an ice cream truck. Some of the people didn't know that ice cream trucks exist. Can you imagine the thoughts running through their heads. Take a television set back to 1920 and maybe get a similar reaction. The truck being very pretty, instead of an ugly box truck blows their minds even more. Since I have 70 different novelties to choose from, that adds to their astonishment.

Many people told me that they didn't believe they heard an ice cream truck until they actually saw me; they thought that someone was artificially creating the music. Some people thought it was strange to easily hear someone else's cellular telephone.

On Monday, I explored more small towns while slowly getting closer to Toledo. Many people wanted to know when I would be back. I was in a town which only has ice cream at the Pawn Shop. When dusk arrived, I found the highway to return to Toledo. During the four days of my road trip, I logged 43 hours of driving. I saw many beautiful landscapes; I met a lot of new people, not knowing that I would see several of them one year later. More than half of the 70 ice cream novelties were sold out. I greatly exceeded the four-day sales totals of the other drivers in Toledo. I'm sure my fuel expense also greatly exceeded theirs. I added 16 counties to my total for the year, bringing it to 80.

Chicago is my favorite American city. Among my personal travels, I have driven in, or visited every major American city except Houston and Phoenix. Considering the relative proximity of Chicago to Toledo, I thought it would be fun to sell ice cream there. The summer of 2010 was winding down and I had not yet driven the truck to Chicago.

Chicago is much closer to Toledo than the Mackinac Bridge, so it made sense to me to add it to my route experience.

On a Saturday in September, I left my house not knowing that I would be sleeping in Chicago that night. I drove my car to Mr. Frosty, loaded the truck for my Saturday and headed to the gas station, still not knowing that I was headed to Chicago. After I departed the gas station, the rain arrived. I started driving west hoping that before too long I would see a break in the clouds. I was psychologically prepared to go to Indiana and then loop around from Michigan back to Toledo. When I reached Indiana, the sky was still dark. I then decided that the day had arrived in which I would sell ice cream in Chicago.

I have several friends in Chicago and called a few to let them know I was headed there in an ice cream truck. I entered the highway and drove to Gary, Indiana before the sky looked good.

The chaotic nature of downtown Chicago dictated that I needed to sell ice cream somewhere else, until night arrived. I found a few places to sell and used my iPod to search the internet for an Open Mic. I love to spread my poetry around to new audiences when possible. After the Open Mic, it was late enough for the downtown Chicago party scene. It was a good night of selling and also for adding fun memories for myself and the few dozen customers I encountered.

My favorite moment occurred when a young woman approached the truck to ask me, "Are you Pineapple 16 ?".

I responded, "Yes I am; are you from Bowling Green ?"

She replied, "No; I'm from Toledo." She was with friends and continued walking during our brief conversation.

I loved that my night driving experiences had made someone specifically think of me, even though we were two states away from northwest Ohio.

Since I was so close to the dairy state, I thought that it would be appropriate to sell ice cream in Wisconsin. On Sunday I sold ice cream in two different Wisconsin counties before returning to Illinois. I did another night in Chicago before heading back to Ohio. Due to a busy schedule in 2011, I did not sell ice cream again in Chicago until 2012.

Sometime during 2011, I told Bob that during the previous year, I sold ice cream in Chicago. He told me that if I ever go back there, to not tell him, so he wouldn't have to worry. He knew about my trip to the Mackinac Bridge the day it happened, but Mackinaw City seems closer to Toledo than Chicago because Michigan borders Toledo. Chicago is also very close to Toledo compared to the places I drove in 2012 and 2013.

By 2011, my departure from northwest Ohio had become a regular occurrence. I visited my sister near Columbus a lot that year and developed many routes in central Ohio. By extending my routes farther south, I was creating smaller versions of a road trip in a typical week.

My August road trips seemed so normal. It was the fourth year for my first weekend of August trip. The trip to northern Michigan involved a lot of familiar territory. It was awesome to see customers 52 weeks after our first meeting. Some of the repeat customer sales were within minutes of being EXACTLY 52 weeks after the first encounter, because I followed the same route. I added a day to that road trip making it five days that I was gone from Toledo. It's like a working vacation.

2012 added more road trip excitement. Since the truck wasn't in Chicago in 2011, I went in June when I saw an opening on the calendar. I also had several sales in Wisconsin. I found a nice neighborhood in northern Illinois at the edge of metro Chicago which had never had an ice cream truck visit before. One of the customers waved me down from her car and after spending all her cash of $6, noticed my sign on the window that says, "CREDIT CARDS"; she then spent another $32 on ice cream.

In 2012, I again made several trips to central and south eastern Ohio, building routes and visiting regular customers who only ever see one ice cream truck. Some of the customers know I'm from Toledo, some of them know my sister lives near Columbus.

I was looking forward to my big trip in mid-August to northern Michigan. All my other plans revolved around that trip. Bob, Brenda and everyone else knew I would be gone from Toledo for several days. I checked the weather forecast a few days before my scheduled departure date and saw a problem. I checked the forecast for Illinois and it looked great. Instead of going north from Toledo, I went west.

The first night was in Chicago and I found another Open Mic at a place named, "Let Them Eat Chocolate".

On Saturday, I returned to the neighborhood I had visited in June and was excited about having a repeat customer in Illinois. I then went straight west across northern Illinois stopping at every small town along that route. A few people noticed my Ohio license plate and asked where I was going. Some people asked if their town was going to be part of my route in the future. I told them, "I'm not typically in this area; today's your lucky day."

If I encountered a larger town, I would just drive straight through while hoping to get just one customer. I always like to add a pin to my map of places where I've sold ice cream. If a town is too big, it takes too long to drive around all the streets. There's also a chance that they already have an ice cream truck serving their needs. If I'm going to add a bunch of miles to the truck, I prefer to find some kid in the middle of nowhere who can't walk down the street to buy ice cream from a gas station. I found out that one of the towns I visited had never had an ice cream truck because the dad told me that while he and his young son were in the yard, the boy heard the ice cream music several blocks away and asked his dad what that sound was. His dad responded, "It sounds like an ice cream truck, but we never get ice cream trucks here." I came around the corner a minute later.

In another town I visited, I was stopped by a family who had a bunch of fresh produce in the back of their van with the door open. I mentioned that I had never seen a zucchini bigger than that. The dad handed it to me and offered me other items. I accepted his generous offer.

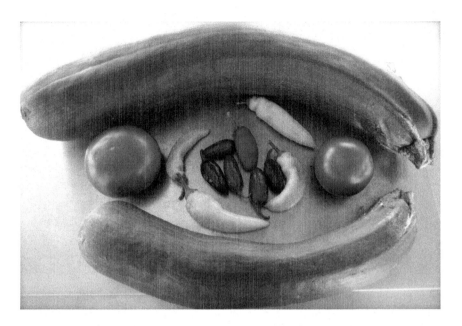

I ate the tomatoes within a day; they weren't going to survive the trek back to Toledo. A few towns later, I encountered a family who after getting their ice cream, the mom stayed near the truck to help the young neighbor girl who came over by herself. She was about six years old and wearing old clothes. She only had one dollar, but wanted something which cost more than that. The woman who stayed to help her, told her to get what she wanted and she then paid the extra amount. I asked her if she liked zucchini. She answered, "Yes, and our garden didn't do well this year."

I reached for the giant zucchini and handed it to her saying, "Here is a gift for you."

As I wandered west across Illinois, I noticed on the map, a village named, "Ohio". It seemed appropriate that I should go there. It was a good visit. During one of the stops, a woman stated that she never saw an ice cream truck in her town before. I responded, "The weird thing is, I've never driven an ice cream truck here before, but I'm from Ohio."

She looked perplexed, which I expected. Her husband then told her about my license plate. I explained my road trip travel plans to them.

I continued west.

Even with the awareness of my own eccentricity, I was still experiencing feelings of surrealism when I reached the Mississippi River in an ice cream truck from the state of Ohio. I was excited about driving in Iowa. One boy told me that he had only ever seen an ice cream truck on the SpongeBob show. A woman in her thirties told me that she had never seen an ice cream truck before. I encountered dozens of ice cream truck rookies.

I so very much love creating that opportunity.

It's a bonus in life, to be appreciated.

Even though Mount Pleasant Iowa is a city, I wanted to sell ice cream there, and considering how far I had traveled from Ohio, it wasn't too much out of the way. I primarily only wanted to have a few customers in Iowa and Missouri before returning to Toledo. I planned on visiting a friend in Quincy Illinois, so that put the Mississippi River in the vicinity of my route.

The reason that I wanted to sell in Mount Pleasant is because, during a personal vacation to Montana in 1993, I stopped there on the way back to Ohio. Its name had a connection to something from my job, and when I couldn't make the connection, I knew that my vacation was a psychological success.

The return home from Missouri involved more ice cream truck rookies. Some of them didn't know how to stop an ice cream truck and it took me a while to adapt to their confusion.

It seems like some people behave as if they think I can read their mind. I need a clear obvious signal that a person wants me to stop.

I drive a lot of miles in a day and can't be stopping for people who are just curious about my presence. I need to know that they want to buy ice cream from me.

During the six days of my Iowa road trip, I drove 1,460 miles during on-duty time of 50 hours. I added 24 sales counties to bring my total that year to 105.

While in Mount Pleasant Iowa, I bought an orange T-shirt bearing its name. I wore it on the first day back in Toledo. When I walked into the office to turn in my money from the trip, Brenda noticed my shirt and said, "You didn't." I responded with a smile, "I did."

I was disappointed about not returning to northern Michigan in 2012, but the trip to Iowa and Missouri was fantastic. It caused me to want to stretch my horizon even farther the following year.

By the time the **2013** season started, I was dating someone whom I had told about my ice cream adventures. She expressed a desire to accompany me on my August road trip. I love it when friends go on a route with me, so that I can share the magic of driving around in an ice cream truck. I'm very glad that my friend Amanda went with me once on my Amish route.

As the 2013 season progressed, I was developing ideas about my August road trip with my new girlfriend; it would have involved more leisure time mixed with the sales. She got a full-time job in June, so as usual, I went by myself. I knew that I wanted to go to Iowa again, but was thinking bigger. I have two friends in Minnesota, so my destination was clear.

I planned for the trip to be 11 or 12 days. I loaded the freezer very tight and full. The first night was just like the previous year, spent in Chicago after performing at the Open Mic at "Let Them Eat Chocolate". On Saturday, I followed the same route across northern Illinois, visiting the same towns 52 weeks after my previous encounter. One of the families remembered me and asked where I was going this time.

I crossed the Mississippi River at a different location than in 2012.

I worked my way north in Iowa toward Minnesota.

One of the towns I visited in Iowa presented an encounter with a police officer who informed me that I needed a separate permit which was not immediately available. He informed me that I **didn't** need to leave, but I could no longer sell anything. I mention that point because of the story about Seville, Ohio in "The Dark Side" chapter.

I enjoyed the scenery which sometimes included visuals of the Mississippi River as I drove north. The first town I encountered in Minnesota brought several people on foot and in cars to the location of my first and only stop in that village. I continued on toward Minneapolis. I spent that night at my friend Jake's house. I met Jake at an Open Mic during a winter vacation while passing through Minneapolis. Jake rode with me the next day as he showed me several good places in Minneapolis to sell ice cream. After a few hours, I said ,"au revoir" to Jake and then continued northwest.

It took two days of ice cream driving to arrive at the home of my other friend in Minnesota. During those two days, I had my picture taken by two different newspaper reporters. I was also interviewed by one of them. The sudden appearance of an ice cream truck in their town was big news. I also found out, that there was social media chatter about an ice cream truck being in the area.

Also during that two-day trek, one of the most interesting stops I've ever had occurred. A 16-year-old boy stopped me and came out to the truck from the left side of the road. He was wearing a cowboy hat and a cowboy tie. If I had been in Texas, I would have thought nothing of it. He bought a popsicle and told me that his brother was coming out to buy something. As he walked away, two young boys came up to the serving window from the right side of the road. I was standing up as they approached, so I couldn't see the house they came from. The four-year-old ordered a $2 item. The two-year-old, who was only wearing a diaper, said, "I'll have the same thing." I pulled the items from the freezer and at that point expected to see a parent headed to the truck. I squatted down to see their house, but nobody else was coming. The older boy handed me $4; I handed them their treats; they returned to their house. Then the cowboy returned to inform me that his brother decided that he didn't want anything.

Their behavior suggests previous ice cream truck experience, while most of the people I encountered in Minnesota made it clear to me that they never get ice cream trucks.

In another town, 13-year-old twin boys stopped me. One brother had $1.50; the other had nothing. The boy with money wanted a Cotton Candy popsicle; its price is $1. He was willing to give his brother the other 50 cents, which is only good for candy. The boy with no money suggested that they buy a Twin Pop and split it; its price is also $1. He also suggested that they spend the other 50 cents on candy. Money boy had his heart set on a Cotton Candy popsicle. They discussed their opposing opinions for a couple of minutes. I was mildly entertained by the sibling conflict until the boy with no money stormed away in frustrated anger. Money boy chased after him trying to apologize. I got back in the driver's seat and drove away. I drove around the corner and was stopped at a daycare center. The teacher came out to the truck with nine very young children. They each spent $1. I was then sold out of Cotton Candy popsicles.

Before leaving that stop, the twins had returned with $2. They told me that they had it figured out. Money boy immediately and confidently ordered a Cotton Candy popsicle. I told him that I just sold the last one. I'm not sure what trivial news could have been worse for him. He had no idea what to do. I pointed out the other items which cost $1. A few minutes went by before he decided on one. His brother bought the same thing. A couple of towns later, I discovered that there **was** one more Cotton Candy popsicle up against the side of the box.

During my ice cream adventures over the years, I have encountered people who told me that they didn't want ice cream because they just ate some. It seemed like a valid reason until I drove along Otter Tail Lake in Minnesota. I had two consecutive stops in which people holding an ice cream cone came out to the truck to buy ice cream. I already mentioned that situation in the "Behavior Modification" chapter. I mention it again because it was during an amazing road trip and so unique.

I was excited when I reached the city where my friend Tami lives. I spent Tuesday and Wednesday night at her house. She and her younger daughter rode with me on Wednesday, pointing out the best places to try ice cream trucking. I sold more in three hours than I would in two days in Ohio on a week day in August.

I again loved having a friend with me, but it was extra special because of having witnesses to the noticeable behavior I saw. What caught my attention is the amount of jaws I saw drop. I noticed some drivers stop their vehicle in awe to watch the ice cream truck drive by. Some people looked as if they were witnessing an alien spaceship fly by.

It was incredible for me to witness their reactions to my presence. I had seen many people stunned before as I drove by in rural areas, but not in a city.

Considering my proximity to North Dakota, of course I headed west after leaving Tami's. My goal was one customer. I went to Fargo and picked a random street. I had one stop with several customers. One of the moms said to me, "Don't be a stranger." She obviously didn't notice my Ohio license plate. I handed her a bumper sticker which advertises this book online, hoping she would discover that my return was unlikely.

(the bumper sticker is Chapter 16 photo)

I drove through a small town south of Fargo with no customers. My next stop was in South Dakota. I had several stops in SD before returning to Iowa.

As I drove across Iowa, more items disappeared from the available menu. I still had dozens of choices and many people commented that there were too many. When I reached the Mississippi River, I still had a long way to go, to get to northwest Ohio. I thought my girlfriend would be eager to see me; I was eager to see her, so I did less wandering and followed a pretty straight path to home. The village of Ohio, Illinois was not on the way to Minnesota, so I put it on my path back to the east. It was nice at that point to see something familiar. It also repeated with good sales.

One of the villages in Illinois is in a county with a strict policy regarding sales of any kind. After a few customers, the sheriff stopped me to inform me about the policy. I asked the sheriff if the policy governed private property. When he asked why I wanted to know, I told him about a man who chased me in his truck to ask if I could come down his dead-end street where they had seen me go by.

The sheriff allowed me to go back to that street and told me not to worry about being on or off the street. NOTE: Please keep this story in mind for comparison while reading about Seville, Ohio in "The Dark Side" chapter. He told me that I would not be able to sell anywhere in that county after that. It was late in the day, so I closed the window and kept driving east so that I would not be gone for 11 or 12 days as originally planned.

My first customers the next day were Joy's daughters in western Indiana. I mentioned Joy in the "Are You Lost ?" chapter. After leaving Joy's house, I followed the same path as I had the previous year for part of my trek across Indiana. I was getting more eager to see my girlfriend and loved surprising her with random visits. She was expecting me on day 11 or 12. I cut the road trip short at ten days and drove to her house.

The ten day road trip added 2,600 miles to the truck during 78 hours of on-duty time. It involved sales in 40 counties in six states.

During my many road trip adventures, **I learned that:**

People recognize ice cream music even when they doubt its existence in their community.

The presence of an ice cream truck is big news in some communities.

I need to allow more reaction time for citizens not familiar with the possibility of an ice cream truck arriving.

Most people don't pay attention to, or care about the fact that I'm from Toledo, Ohio.

People who are aware of my base location, honor my presence in a way which makes everyone feel special.

I wish more people could regularly experience both sides of the relationship that I share with the customers whom I encounter on a road trip.

Bowling Green, Ohio

Bowling Green, Ohio is the seat of Wood County, which is the next county south of Lucas, where Mister Frosty is based. It takes less than half an hour to drive there from Toledo. Several Toledo ice cream trucks roam the streets of B.G. during any given week of the season, during the day. Bowling Green is the home of the National Tractor Pull every August. I don't know if other drivers have sold ice cream during that event, but I never have. Bowling Green is also home to The American Legion's Buckeye Boys State. There are also many other events at various times held in Bowling Green. I have occasionally sold ice cream during a few of them. As a citizen enjoying the offerings of a community, I appreciate the Black Swamp Arts Festival held in September. The Arts Festival hinders my ice cream sales though.

The primary reason that I drive there, is because of Bowling Green State University. Due to a regulation of unknown explanation, I am not permitted to sell ice cream on most of the property governed by BGSU. One time I was sent to three different offices to obtain permission, before finding out that it wasn't going to happen. Apparently, there is an entity on campus which is uncomfortable with the occasional sales of Ninja Turtle popsicles to the students. I have received conflicting information about the permissibility to sell ice cream near the football stadium.

Even though I am not allowed inside the main campus area, I have good sales in the housing areas near campus which are occupied by BGSU students. The best times to sell those students ice cream is after dusk.

Bowling Green is special for several reasons. Its proximity to Toledo makes it very easy to visit frequently. I have enjoyed many situations there which have not occurred elsewhere.

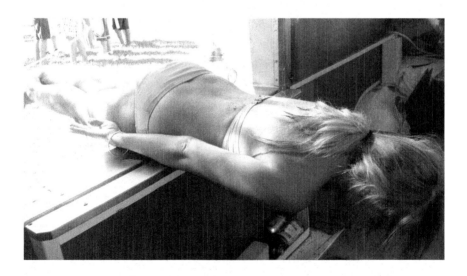

The latest sale I ever had was 4:30 a.m. It was the night of BGSU Homecoming. After the football game, everyone is in more of a party mood than usual. On that record night, I was busy until 4:00, and then it started slowing down.

I have also sold ice cream to many people in Bowling Green when it was 53 degrees and pouring rain. The key component in that scenario is that it was dark. Rain keeps a lot of daytime people inside, but if people are out on the town for the night, rain doesn't matter. In B.G., it seems that there is no deterrent.

There have been several occasions in which I have sold ice cream in B.G. when it was below 40 degrees. One of my B.G. nights occurred when the daytime high temperature reached 41. For a while my record low temperature for selling was 32. I loved that my record was in B.G. I broke that record though outside of B.G. on April 20th, 2013 when the late evening temperature dropped to 29.

My many successful visits to Bowling Green inspired me to explore other campus areas such as Ohio State University and Ohio University. I also have sold ice cream near another dozen universities.

BGSU students also repeatedly pointed out to me in 2011 that I needed to accept credit cards as a payment option. I had previously explored that possibility, but the costs were too high for a seasonal situation. By 2012 though, smart phone applications made credit card acceptance easy and affordable. My eight-year-old cellular telephone worked very well, but I needed the internet with me. I bought a smart phone right before the season started in 2012 and credit card sales that year justified its purchase.

Another aspect I have enjoyed about Bowling Green is that so many people know who I am. Even though I enjoy exploring new territory all the time, and there's always a friendly acceptance when arriving at the home of a regular customer. It's a different kind of comfort to be welcomed by strangers when cruising around B.G. There are many times when I see people I personally know, but many times I don't recognize the people whom I see yelling, "Pineapple 16" as I drive by.

Another of the great reasons why Bowling Green works so well for selling ice cream is the layout of the downtown bar scene related to the location of campus. There are over one dozen bars located on one block in the center of downtown. After 1:00 a.m., it is best to find a parking spot in front of one of them to enjoy the frequency of random bar-hoppers walking by.

Some of the college students I know like to participate in selling ice cream. When I typically receive free assistance, it is two girls who beam with friendliness and energy to attract more customers to the truck. They experience great satisfaction and pride by helping me get more sales. Some of the people also want to ride around town to help sell to the crowds at parties.

Around the time that the bars close, a giant migration occurs between downtown and campus. I often get more sales by being along the route which most of them traverse on foot.

The movie theater at the mall in B.G. charges a lot less than theaters in metropolitan Toledo. I sometimes take a two-hour break to see a movie when sales are typically slow. There have also been times in which I am in other places far from B.G. selling ice cream until dusk. If I can arrive in Bowling Green between 11:30 p.m. and 1:00 a.m. then it is worth the effort to do so.

While visiting Bowling Green, **I have learned that:**

Campus areas are great for selling ice cream.

Selling ice cream at three in the morning is no big deal.

It's never too cold to sell ice cream from a truck.

Primarily, college students are the best customers. They still exhibit the excitement, exuberance and pure joy of getting ice cream from a truck. They also are adults and have their own money. They are still awake at three in the morning allowing for ice cream sales to go far beyond the schedule of the sun.

The Dark Side

Most of the aspects of driving an ice cream truck involve positive conditions. It seems that the public's reaction to the presence of an ice cream truck also brings about smiles, cheers and other ways of expressing joy and happiness, MOST of the time.

From my perspective, a few negatives are the continual uncertainty of sales, the craziness of the weather, and the potential to meet people who have no regard for others outside their own immediate concerns.

The most common opponent which I have encountered, is someone working in a concession stand, who thinks that giving the public an opportunity to buy a popsicle greatly jeopardizes their ability to sell one of the members of a crowd another hot dog. Even though I do not sell what they are selling and vice versa, they feel highly threatened by my presence, even when I arrive at the end of a game, which is the reason the crowd exists. A few of them have been polite in the way that they express their thoughts about the presence of an ice cream truck, but for the most part, they are rude, bullish, obnoxious and ignorant. I've managed to have slightly-intelligent conversations with a few of them.

I've pointed out that McDonald's probably doesn't like that Burger King is sitting right next door selling the exact same kind of food, but that's the way free enterprise works. That's the way America works.

My niece was riding with me one day and thoroughly enjoyed my debate with a man at a public park who ended up creating more sales for me by continuing his argument that I should leave. There was a baseball game at the park, so he was selling hot dogs. I drove into the park to see if anyone wanted ice cream and people from both sides of the park came to the truck. Half the people were watching the game, and the others were just enjoying the park. The narrow parking area was between the picnic/playground area and the ball diamond. The hot dog vendor wanted to deny EVERYONE the opportunity to buy ice cream from me.

I typically arrive at a scene like that, sell ice cream to the first bunch that shows up and if I don't see someone else approaching the truck, I leave. His desire for a verbal victory against me, kept me sitting there much longer, allowing more people to have enough time to decide that they wanted ice cream.

Some of the concessionaires who decide to act like a bully possibly think that the driver of an ice cream truck has an inferior intelligence compared to theirs. When they see my spider hat upon my head, they probably gain confidence that their argument will be unchallenged; I relish those moments.

There are jurisdictions outside Ohio where I have obtained a vendor's permit to sell, however, if I am confronted with any resistance while outside Ohio, I vehemently respond to their desire for my absence. The standard mobile vendor's permit which is issued each year by the county health department is valid on any public road in all 88 counties of Ohio. This includes most public parks and other properties payed for by taxpayers. If I am at one of those locations, I will strongly defend my right to be there.

In Ohio, ice cream trucks are not permitted to vend in State Parks or Metro Parks because of litter. I was also informed by the manager of an apartment complex, that we are banned for the same reason.

I myself have seen kids rip the wrapper off their treats and drop the wrapper onto the ground. I carry a large cardboard box in the truck, which I replace several times a week, to use as a garbage can. I often ask customers if they would like to use it.

Police officers have caused many problems during my ice cream trucking. Some of them have been off-duty while bullying me.

The first such instance occurred while driving down a dead-end street in a village I would visit once a week. When I drive the truck on a street with a 25 MPH speed limit, I typically travel 16-18 MPH.

On the day of my encounter with the off-duty Ohio state patrol officer, I traveled 18 MPH past his house. His house is about halfway down the 500-feet long road with his state issued patrol car sitting in his driveway.

I turned around at the end, and as I began back toward his house, he was coming out to the street. My first thought is, "That man wants to buy ice cream." He angrily approached the truck as I slowed down to greet him.

He demanded, "YOU NEED TO SLOW DOWN."

I responded, "Isn't the speed limit 25 ?"

The officer's reply: "You were going faster than that."

At this point, a man with two young children approached the truck from a house across the street from the officer.

I asked the officer, "Did you have your RADAR gun on ?"

Officer responds, "I'm trained to estimate speed."

My response was, "Then you need to go back to training cuz I was going 18."

Officer's response in front of his neighbor children, "You're an asshole !!" He then walked back to his house.

In a subdivision at the edge of a village near the city of Toledo, another off-duty police officer started walking to the street as I approached his house in a neighborhood which I drive through about once in a three-week period. He told me that I needed to leave immediately and never come back because he didn't move out there to hear ice cream music. He added to his statement that it was a private street. When I asked if there were signs indicating that it is private, he responded, "I'm a deputy sheriff. Do I need to call someone ?" He then walked back to his house. Since he wasn't buying ice cream, I turned the music back up and continued driving about 18 MPH. When I reached the end of the street where a bicycle trail crosses, I asked the cyclists if they knew about the status of the street being public or private. The one man told me that the residents pay a neighborhood fee, but the streets are public.

Three weeks later, I confirmed that when I was stopped by a customer a few houses away from the deputy's house. I told him what happened during my previous visit. He told me that several of his neighbors didn't move there to hear the deputy's dog barking all the time.

I had another encounter which was far less dramatic with two off-duty officers. I find it interesting that the occupation of certain individuals makes them feel more comfortable bullying someone else. I also had a concession stand worker at a public school track meet inform me that her neighbor was the principal of the school when she was trying to convince me that I needed to leave the premises. I've been told by a police officer that I am allowed to sell at public schools because tax-payer money pays for the school. Private schools can kick me out with no debate.

Haskins, Ohio

Even though I have a mobile vending permit valid on any public road in Ohio, many villages and small cities want money for themselves. They require a permit issued by their police department. Most of them are about $25 annually. Some of them are much higher.

The village of Haskins, Ohio issues a FREE permit. They ONLY require the permit so that they have a record of who is visiting their village. The permit that Haskins issues is valid for 90 days, however they only require an ice cream truck driver to obtain it once a year. When I first started selling ice cream in Haskins, I was stopped by an officer at some point and informed of their policy. I was not cited for having already sold ice cream. At the beginning of each season after that, I would obtain a new permit from the police station.

At the beginning of my fourth year of visiting Haskins, I stopped at the police station, but I learned that I needed to get there before 4:00. I drove around selling ice cream and returned the following week a little earlier. By that point the police officer in charge of issuing me the permit knew who I was. The problem occurred the following year.

I tried to get to the police station by 4:00, but failed to do so. When I approached the station, I saw the police car in front. Since it was a little after 4:00, I thought that it meant the officer had gone home for the day in his personal vehicle. I drove by with the ice cream music at full volume. I reached the street with regular customers less than one minute later. At the first stop, Officer Brian Chambers pulled up behind me. He stood by the front of his car and watched me sell ice cream to two children. Brian then walked up to my window and cited me for selling without a permit.

He compared my driving by the police station with the music playing, to a slap in the face. It's as if he was telling me that it was rude of me to not stop, and he took it personally. I interrupted my selling, followed him back to the station and obtained the permit four minutes later. The following few weeks, I passed out flyers to the adults I sold ice cream to in Haskins, informing them of the situation. My hope was that the residents being aware of the strange situation, would cause them to come to my defense and let their mayor know that the citation was stupid.

I knew that it was unlikely to happen, but at least some of them would know why I disappeared after losing my case.

After a few weeks, I was convicted and had to pay $85.

The facts are: Haskins bends their own rule for ice cream trucks. Their free permit is so they know who is in their village. Officer Chambers, who cited me, **already knew who I was**. He testified in Mayor's court that he had issued me the permit during the two previous years.

Since I was not trying to avoid the cost of a permit, I found the situation to be illogical. Even though my permit was valid for the rest of the year, I never returned to Haskins to sell ice cream again.

Seville, Ohio is a town I visited for the first time in 2013. I was passing through Seville from Medina to Lodi. I noticed a small sub-division off the main road, so I figured that a quick check of ice cream interest would be worthwhile. It made two kids happy and gave me this story. As I turned into the neighborhood, a police cruiser had just passed me going the opposite direction. Upon entering the neighborhood, I was stopped by two children within one minute. Their house was on the left side of the street. They ran across the street, looked at the multitude of options available and told me they would be right back after obtaining money. While they were looking at the many choices, the police cruiser pulled up behind me; the officer stayed in his car.

My experience with the Haskins police made me wonder why he was sitting there without approaching me.

Instead of informing me of a possible law violation, he wanted to witness me committing a crime, instead of preventing one.

Since the children went inside to get money, I backed into their driveway. That reduces danger by having them run across the street again. Since I was on private property, the policeman drove down the street, turned around, and waited for me. I sold ice cream to the two kids in their driveway, **which the officer witnessed**. As soon as I left the driveway, the policeman pulled up next to me, exited his car, and asked me if I had a permit. I began to grab the mobile vendor's permit when he pointed out that he was referring to the permit issued by the village of Seville.

I informed him that I didn't know that one was required. He told me that he knew I didn't have one, because no one had one. He told me that the police chief would be upset if he knew that I wasn't receiving a citation. He also said to me, "You need to leave town...**NOW**". I asked him if the street I was headed toward, looped around to exit the neighborhood. He said that it did. We parted ways. I went around the corner and there were two families standing near the street. I had the music off at that point but figured that they heard me when I was on the previous street and were waiting to buy ice cream. I stopped near them and asked if that's why they were standing there. One of the dads told me that they were just chatting, but since I was there, they would like to buy ice cream. I informed them that the police officer said I needed a permit to sell on the streets of their town. The other dad told me that I could park in their driveway and they would get some money. Before the children even looked at the choices, the police officer had returned. He stopped near the driveway and I walked out to talk with him.

He was obviously angry as he said, "I told you to leave town."

We then discussed the difference between selling on a public street and selling on private property. The officer **claimed** that there was no difference. He also informed me that the man's driveway I was parked in was the best friend of the police chief. He again mentioned that the chief would be upset that he didn't cite me.

I wonder why he didn't cite me if he actually had anything to cite me for. After he told me that the fine would be close to $200, I told him that I would not sell them anything. He told me that he was going to follow me out of town.

I told the families that I was banned from serving them. I left as the officer did follow me more than a mile to the edge of town.

I find the contrast between this story and the two occurrences during my road trip to be intriguing.

During my road trip, I was driving an out-of-state vehicle in Iowa and allowed to stay in the village as long as I didn't sell any more. In Illinois, I was allowed to sell to one more customer without a permit.

The Interrogation

Logic dictates that a larger crowd of people will generate more sales than a small group of people. I had several experiences selling ice cream to the boys at Buckeye Boys State. Boys State and Girls State is a week-long experience for high school students between their junior and senior years. Boys State is close to Toledo, so several visits are easy for me. Many of the boys in attendance never have an opportunity for an ice cream truck in their hometown. After having good sales results at Boys State, I thought it would be good to give the girls a chance to buy ice cream from a truck. Buckeye Girls State is much farther from Toledo at Mount Union College in Alliance, Ohio. There are fewer girls than boys in Ohio's version, but I expected enthusiasm for the ice cream opportunity presented to them. The greater distance from Toledo would also allow me to explore other towns in between to find new customers. My experience at Boys State made it easier to know when to be there and which part of campus to be located.

After arriving at Mount Union, I drove through campus, barely seeing any people. I parked the truck and walked to the information center to hopefully gain insight as to when and where the girls would be for free time to be able to buy ice cream. No information was available. When I was walking back to the truck, parked on a public street next to campus, a man asked if I was its driver. He asked for my identification. He said that we needed to wait for the highway patrol to show up; I was fine with that, however, if I had known that it was going to take more than half an hour, I wouldn't have been fine. As the security guard, he could have informed me that Mount Union was a private school, end of story. Instead of such a simple ending, we waited. We waited for the officers to get dressed.

It was 4:00 p.m. What's that about ?

Finally, three female officers show up wearing T-shirts which say, "Ohio

Highway Patrol" and begin interrogating me about my presence there. They asked me many stupid, irrelevant questions. One of the questions was, "Does that truck use Diesel ?" The security guard asked me more than once why I went to the information center. They insinuated that the only reason I was there, was to abduct and/or rape girls. They wanted me to think about the situation from their perspective: "We're in charge of all these girls and an ice cream truck shows up all of a sudden."

I'm wondering if they realize that EVERYWHERE an ice cream truck goes, it shows up all of a sudden.

It's a good thing that I didn't ask them to THINK, about it from my perspective: "There's 900 people in one location who possibly want ice cream from a truck. If only 5% of them actually buy ice cream, that's a good visit."

Logic and common sense dictate that if someone were to be abducted in the most easily noticeable vehicle on the road, 900 witnesses would complicate the plan. The security guard asked if I had a daughter. After my response of, "No; I have nieces.", he replied, "It's not the same." My wonderment is, "What's not the same ?". If his niece is abducted, he's not going to care about it ? I added to my reply, "I've never been married and I have no kids." My personal information which they all just received, matches many homosexual men. Since I informed them of my presence at Boys State, why didn't they alert the people there ? Either the security guard or the highway patrol had the Alliance police department call Bob on the telephone to ask if one of his ice cream trucks had been stolen. Bob knows I drive all over the place, so he was not alarmed when he learned how far Alliance was from Toledo. Since that incident, I only go to Boys State during that week.

Extortion

I have only experienced an attempted extortion one time. It was during my Kalida fireworks event. The fireworks were displayed at a golf course three miles outside the village. Many people park along the four different roads which surround the site to watch the show. Three of the roads have agriculture fields across from the golf course. The other road is lined with houses.

During my third time at the event, while slowly driving on the road lined with houses, a man approached me on a golf cart. He was associated with the golf course. He was upset that I was making money by taking advantage of the fireworks show. He told me that if I didn't donate money to him, he was going to notify the sheriff of my non-compliance. I'm not sure exactly what he tried to threaten me with; the whole conversation was very sudden and surprising.

I had a mobile vendor's permit allowing me to sell on a public road. I wasn't on his golf course property. He was illegally driving a motorized vehicle on that public road. I didn't give him any money. I drove past the sheriff several times. I never heard anything more about it.

Perks ? Yes.

One of the cities I occasionally visit for campus activities has several street vendors selling various hot foods. Of course each of those vendors has to obtain a permit from the city. Since I usually assume no extra permit is required for me, I didn't inquire about the local ordinance. One or two vendors were upset about an ice cream truck showing up. Of course, THEY were NOT selling ice cream. I was approached and asked if I had a permit issued by the city. I told them that I did not. After a few visits, over the course of more than a year, I was also asked by more than one police officer, if I had a permit issued by the city.

One of the officers told me where the building is to obtain a permit. This occurred near midnight. He told me that I could continue selling that night, but would need to get a permit the next day. I was typically in the town on the weekend for one or two nights and then not near it for a while, especially during business hours. Bob will pay for the permits; I have to do the paperwork and give him the receipts. When I finally returned to that city during business hours, I went to obtain a permit. I learned that since I am primarily selling dairy products, I don't need a permit. If I were selling eggs, I also would not need a permit. The clerk showed me the ordinance which dictates the exemption for those selling dairy or eggs. I informed the clerk that I also sell popsicles which contain no milk. Since they are a low percentage of my available products, I was still exempt. I'm guessing the exemption was put into effect a century ago and never altered.

I asked the clerk to give me a photocopy of the exemption clause because I knew that the police didn't know about it. There were two or three times after that, in which I showed the exemption clause to police who asked me if I had a permit. Since that time, the police have been aware of my special privileges. There are occasions in that city in which the college students have street parties. The local vendors would like to move their mobile food wagons to the block of the street party; they are NOT allowed to do so. I am allowed to drive on those streets during the party because I am driving an ICE CREAM TRUCK. Since many people were concerned about whether or not I had a permit, I became aware of the privileged status of an ice cream truck in that town. I also made the police aware of it.

During one of my visits, as I was leaving town, I was stopped at a gas station at the edge of town loading up on diesel fuel. A local resident about age 60 asked about my ice cream sales. His curiosity was not because he wanted to buy anything from me. It was because he was not aware of my exemption. I told him about it and he refused to believe me. I asked if the ordinance had changed in the last half a year. He said that it hadn't. He was CONVINCED that I was breaking the law by selling ice cream in that town without the permit required by other food vendors.

I learned that:

Not everyone is in love with the appearance of an ice cream truck.

Many police officers like to bully the public whether they are on duty or not.

Some police officers recognize the bigger picture that an ice cream truck isn't a threat to the structure of our society.

Many people will debate rules and philosophies they know nothing about, with an ice cream truck driver.

Hints & Statistics

As a potential ice cream truck customer, there are several things which could be helpful to remember. I list these because I have noticed that some people do not realize some of them.

#1: Ice cream truck drivers can **NOT** read your mind.

If you want the driver to stop, you need to make it obvious.

Waving your arms back and forth is a great method.

Holding up money is a great method.

Screaming, "WAIT, I WANT ICE CREAM" is a great method.

Standing there staring is **NOT** effective.

#2: Ice cream truck drivers are continually looking in several directions. We are scanning. If you don't see the driver notice you, the driver probably did **not** notice you.

#3: People wave at the ice cream truck **ALL** the time, without wanting to buy ice cream. Refer to Guideline **#1**

#4: There are variances in how many miles an ice cream truck travels in a day. If you live outside a large city where ice cream trucks are based, then the truck is not going to travel at only four miles per hour past your house.

If you want the truck to stop, RUN toward the road and signal the driver to stop. If you then need to acquire money, do that next.

#5: We don't want a bunch of pennies. It would be nice to be able to spend lots of time counting small coins, but it's highly inefficient. Most people are unaware that there is a federal guideline against using more than 25 pennies for a single purchase; that's why larger coins exist.

I had customers use a $100 bill to purchase less than $5 worth; that's also ridiculous.

#6: If you're at a sporting event which doesn't have an ice cream truck in attendance and then one shows up, you should immediately go to the truck. It's probably not going to be there very long.

#7: If you're following an ice cream truck while traveling slower than the speed limit, and you're on a flat road with no curves and no oncoming traffic, please **go around it.**

#8: If you like the service provided by an ice cream truck, please consider offering the driver a tip. 25 cents is a nice bonus; of course a dollar is awesome. Food is also an excellent tip.

If you are an ice cream truck driver, welcome to my book; I hope you enjoy it. I offer these tips in the hopes that they will increase your sales.

#1: EXPLORE. Try a new road in your regular area. Try a new area.
Try a different time of the week in an area you already know.
Drive slowly through the parking lot of an auto repair shop or other places where men working are not in air conditioned comfort.

#2: SLOW DOWN or STOP near a corner. Drive around the block twice if it looks favorable. Park at fast food restaurants because the employees want ice cream from you.

#3: Drive after dusk in friendly neighborhoods and downtown areas where crowds gather for a night out. When the children are in bed, the adults are playing. Adults have their own money.

#4: Drive in rural areas where farmers are. Find the smallest town you can, and explore every street.

#5: Get rolls of half-dollars and two-dollar bills from your bank. Customers love them. They are good for emergencies when you're low on quarters or dollar bills.

#6: When sales go down in July or August, drive somewhere else. Stop driving the same area repeatedly. The end of the season is great for finding new customers to know where to go the following year.

#7: Drive down DEAD END roads. Those people want ice cream too and they have two chances to stop you.

#8: If you can't accept credit cards as payment, you're missing a lot of sales.

I learned:

Most people don't understand how complicated it is to be successful at selling ice cream from a truck for an entire season.

Many people are bad with simple hand signals.

Some children have their own debit cards.

The deployment of an airbag can cause serious damage or injury if you're too close to it. The video "Airbag deployment kills spider hat" shows how I learned that. It was not while driving the truck.

It was on the property of Mister Frosty while a junk vehicle had its airbags activated.

KEEP SMALL CHILDREN OUT OF THE FRONT SEAT.
DISABLE THE DRIVER'S SIDE AIRBAG if you have shorter legs causing you to sit very close to your steering wheel.

Statistics

I spend about $5,600 on fuel each year to drive the truck about 28,000 miles.

There have been several days which I finished with less money than I started with, because my sales did not justify my fuel expense. On those days, I was only rewarded by the joy of creating smile opportunities or possibly a good photo opportunity.

There have been a few days in which I went home with more money than I seemed to earn. Some of those days were over 14 hours long, but those hours are usually fun. It only seems like work during the last couple of hours of selling to a fireworks crowd.

The most I drove an ice cream truck in one day is 464 miles. It was a Wednesday. I started in Toledo and finished in Athens.

The latest time for my last stop of the day was 4:24 a.m. in Bowling Green. Saturday night parties lasted a while. I had two other nights which lasted until 4:00 a.m. Those two nights were at O.S.U.

The latest time in which I had my first stop of the day is 11:30 p.m. It was a Saturday in April. 55 degrees for a high temperature with cloudiness, made the DAY not good for selling ice cream. On a Saturday NIGHT, the weather is less relevant.

I have gained sales by being stopped for various reasons. I have gained many customers by stopping to look at my map, or to use Wi-Fi.

I have gained several customers by stopping to photograph a scene.

I had two occurrences of people buying ice cream while we were waiting for a train.

I sold ice cream once while stopped at a red light. The customer was a passenger in a car on my left. He quickly ran around to the serving window and back to the car before the light was green.

I gained several customers by being directed to a street by a man who saw me pulled over by a police car. The police officer was inquiring about my previous stop and agreed with the other man that I should follow him to get more customers. The previous stop was private property and I was told to leave. As I left, some children stopped me at the end of the driveway of the country club. Since I was at the edge of the property, and not yet on the street, someone called the police. I told the children that I needed to be on the street and they walked the extra 20 feet to buy their ice cream. The officer didn't cite me, but needed to check the situation.

The coldest environment I sold ice cream in was 29 degrees. The high that day was 43. It was a Saturday in April. I didn't start selling until 5 p.m.

The hottest environment was 106 degrees. It was July 4th, so plenty of people were outside partying.

I have had many non-human customers. At least 50 dogs have been my customer; one of them had its own money as it walked up to the truck with a dollar bill in its mouth. I've had three horse customers at two stops. All three horses received popsicles. One macaque named Lily has been a repeat customer. Clyde the donkey is a regular customer.

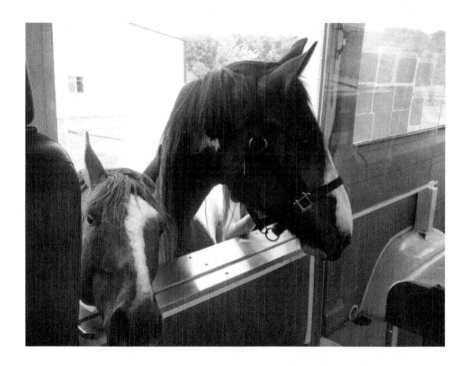

Many people have offered items for barter, typically because of them having no cash. I didn't accept every trade which was offered. I rarely was satisfied with the trades I made; I primarily made the trades to help the customers. There were two times in which teenagers at their school were waiting for their rides home when I arrived, and one of them was creative enough to suggest a trade. Others in the vicinity took advantage of my deal-making because they also possessed something they would trade for ice cream. During the first of those two, most of the kids traded pencils or similar items for any $1.00 item. The kids at the second school traded candy which they received from cheerleaders.

My favorite barter was for acorn squash from one of my regular Amish customers.

Other items offered for barter which may, or may not have been traded, include: bandages, basketballs, beer, condoms, ice cream coupons from a restaurant, ice cream coupons from a school, erasers, food from a restaurant, food not from a restaurant, kiss, flash of skin, stamps, telephone call, washing the truck, and working in the truck.

Many people are lazy and lack the imagination of those offering a trade. I've been asked dozens of times by those lazy people if anything was free. I would love to see those people walk into random stores and ask the cashier if anything is free.

There was an occasion while driving a regular Tuesday route, in which I was on a street near a recurring customer's house. I was in a good mood and happy to see someone who had previously bought something from me. The teenager didn't have money that day and was with several friends walking down the street. One of the friends asked about free stuff. My good mood and my realization of the opportunity to teach a simple lesson caused me to say this, "I will give each of you one free lollipop if within ten seconds any one of you correctly spells 'voila'." About one second elapsed when one of the boys calmly, yet quickly spelled it, "V, O, I, L, A".

I pointed at him and said to the others, "There's your hero."

I then grabbed their rewards and handed them out.

I have made similar offers to kids if they could correctly tell me certain state capitals. I always ask the same one first, because most people who claim to know all the capitals, forget Missouri's. I've taught many children that Jefferson City is the capital of Missouri. I love to add to their ability to distinguish it from similar pairs of initials by also teaching them that Jackson is the capital of Mississippi.

If they enjoy other trivia, I point out that Jackson is on the $20 bill and Mississippi was the 20th state to enter the union.

The earliest in the season I drove is March 27th. The latest in the season is October 14th. I average 10 days per season not driving the truck.

Almost all days off are because of very bad weather or truck problems.

Some bad weather days have involved me driving because I know I can get customers in certain places.

I learned:

Any situation which causes an ice cream truck to be stopped can lead to more sales.

People who have no money, get very creative with bartering to possibly obtain ice cream from a truck.

Bad weather does not prevent people from buying ice cream.

Most people believe that hot weather increases ice cream truck sales; they are wrong.

The clock is irrelevant when ice cream desire exists.

September

The typical ice cream truck season in northwest Ohio starts late March and goes through September. Occasionally early October is included. During the beginning of the year, everyone is excited about the ice cream truck arriving. Sales in April and May are generally very good if it's not raining; June is variable. Since many customers are children, the summer break from school makes sales days longer. The sun setting later also helps with long sales days. After the fireworks shows of early July, sales continue to drop steadily the rest of the season. If drivers continue to drive in the same areas repeatedly, many customers no longer are excited about ice cream truck visits. August is an accentuation of July, and excitement is more challenging to discover. Since sales drop so much in late summer, many ice cream drivers stop selling after Labor Day. I struggled with low sales numbers during the late season my first few years, because like most drivers, I focused on selling ice cream to children.

2007 was a huge year for the evolution of my sales strategy. When I started selling at night, I realized that September brings huge potential for sales because of college students.

I also realized that since late season sales are pitiful in areas that were drained of excitement prior to September, it's best to explore completely new areas. I love finding the excitement. New customers ask me, "Where have you been all summer ?". When that happens, I know to add that area to my plans for the early part of the next season. Some of my best route areas throughout the season are places which I first drove in a previous September.

I first went to Athens in September and learned that I need to go there regularly. My first sales in Chicago and Wisconsin were in September, but it wouldn't work well to go there often.

Along with selling to the college students at night, another good strategy is taking advantage of the activities near high schools. Cross Country meets, football games and other athletic competitions draw crowds in areas not always served by a concession stand.

Bob lets the inventory get much lower by late August because of poor September sales. As September progresses, many of the trucks are parked until spring. The remaining inventory is moved to trucks still operating. Bob and I have had to work out different strategies in the last several years because my September sales are much greater than those of other drivers. I have had several of my better sales days occur in September.

During September 2013, I had my second-best sales day of my ice cream man career.

Some of my sales days in September are poor due to honoring the connection I have with regular customers. I dislike abandoning my best customers due to non-existent sales along the rest of a regular route.

I will drive many miles with zero sales to be able to continue selling to my regulars.

As an artist, I enjoy having extra time away from the truck as September days are shorter. With the cooler weather, fewer adults want ice cream, so it's primarily back to the children after school. The sun sets sooner, so sales days are brief, except for Thursday, Friday and Saturday nights, when I am near campus until three in the morning.

September brings a higher recurrence of the question, "**What do you do in the winter ?**". My answer is, "It varies."

The first two winters involved having a full-time job because I barely made any money during the season. I've gotten better at having greater sales during the season and spending my time earning money. Driving the truck every possible day during the season leaves little time to spend money.

More than one winter involved writing this book. I work on other creative projects too. My photography, poetry, cruzadex puzzle making, and video productions receive more attention. I spend more time visiting family and friends. If I have extra money, I travel. I do some freelance work.

Another fun activity in winter, is chess with more than two players. I designed an eight-man chess board based on other boards I have seen which use three or four players. I also adapted the rules so that games don't last forever. I've played dozens of four-man games. I've only played eight-man once so far.

A couple different winters involved me performing in community theater. My most challenging role was portraying Dr. Ginsberg in Agatha Christie's, "The Patient".

In November 2009, I performed in some scenes in the movie, "Separation Anxiety", which was filmed in Ohio.

In November 2012, I was part of a medical mission team to Tanzania; I was recruited to document the mission.

I've also done other volunteer work in the autumn and winter.

My largest puzzle contains 2560 words; it took me over ten years to create.

While driving the ice cream truck around for several years, I have seen hundreds of personalized license plates. I have so far written two poems using only words from license plates which I have photographed. To see those on Youtube, search for "License Plate Poem #1" or "License Plate Poem #2"

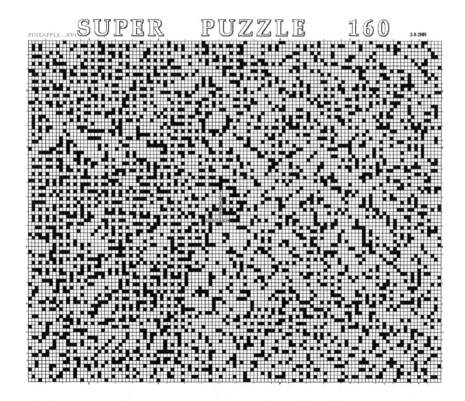

SUPER PUZZLE 160

PINEAPPLE...XVI

2-8-2009

I learned that:

September is great for exploring and learning new territory.

A new school year brings many sales opportunities which most ice cream drivers ignore.

Many people greatly miss ice cream truck visits during times when they can't receive them.

Driving an ice cream truck is highly rewarding in many ways.

Since Santa Claus is only briefly accessible in December, many children find great joy when they can interact with a person they interpret as only bringing them smiles and delicious treats.

I have been inspired to:

Write poems and create videos based on my ice cream truck experiences.

Explore many different sales opportunities.

Explore different cultures.

I have made many friends, met hundreds of very interesting people, and made thousands of people smile just by driving a truck which has the words "ICE CREAM" printed on the side.

I have enjoyed many ice cream truck adventures.

I plan to explore other life adventures and will miss driving an ice cream truck.

I will miss:

Experiencing the uninhibited expressed joy, of new customers.

Sharing stories with regular customers.

College tailgate parties and other campus fun.

Being a hero to that one kid whom I randomly encounter in the middle of nowhere.

I might return.

I am grateful that Bob allowed me so much freedom and trusted me in many ways. Part of that trust was conveyed by sharing information with me and knowing that he wasn't wasting his breath.

I am grateful that my love of driving created awesome memories for me and thousands of other people.

Thank you Dad, Diana, Erica, Jackie and Kathy for editing suggestions.

Thank you Melanie for helping me, and encouraging me, and repeating that process in the continuation of creating this book.

My Day was made more *AWESOME* by
Pineapple....XVI & the Ice Cream Truck
facebook.com / PineappleXVI
facebook.com / LessonsFromAnIceCreamTruck

Quotations

One the many enjoyable aspects about driving an ice cream truck, is hearing the excitement, the amazement, the wonder, the appreciation, and the pure joy in the voices of the many people I encounter.

There were many circumstances which I regret letting slip away without documentation. Some of the quotes which I documented, occurred before I knew I was writing this book. I kept track of a few because they were special. After accepting the responsibility of writing this book, I tried to document fun quotes more often. I listed one of them on the first page and will mention it again to start this chapter.

Bob told me several times that some children use money for the first time when buying ice cream from a truck. I witnessed interaction between children and their parents many times with the parent explaining how to use their money. If the child was to receive change, some parents would ask the child how much change they should receive before I started giving it to them. Some parents send their children to the truck while they observe from the front door. Some children are completely independent during their ice cream purchases.

The memory which triggers my sentimentality and causes me to tear up a little bit, is from hearing the honest direct words from the sweet voice of a seven-year-old girl:

"I never used money before; I don't know how it works."

I still remember exactly where that occurred.

Some of the other quotes also burned their location into my memory.

One of those happened while approaching a traffic light at an intersection in a rural area. There is a small collection of houses all four directions from the intersection. For a few years, I went down that road about twice a month during the summer. It was always on a Tuesday. One day a man in his late 30s ran out to the truck waving his arms while I was driving by. He seemed frantic and eager in his quest. When I stopped, I wasn't even able to stand next to the freezer yet before he announced his desire:

"I have $1.85 and need chocolate !!"

I told him that the Fudge Bar is $1.25. He put all his money on the serving window and waited for me to hand him the Fudge Bar. He was happy.

I do not remember the circumstances of some of these quotes. Here are several which popped up various places:

"When the ice cream truck comes…it's the BEST sound"

6-year-old girl

"I knew the ice cream truck would come someday"

12-year-old boy

"What took you so long to get here ?"

12-year-old girl

"I've been waiting for you, my whole life"

woman in mid 30s in Sylvania Township

"How did you find our town ?"

woman in Clark County during my first visit

"We're in the process of begging our parents for money"

high school boy

"Our financial support is on the way"

mom with kids referring to her husband

"I have a college degree and I just begged my mom for money for the ice cream truck"

"You should just give him your whole purse"

6-year-old to his mom while she was digging for $4, perhaps meaning they could get more ice cream if I received ALL her money

"Great timing; I'd thought you'd never get here"

woman in early 60s on bike trail near the road in a small village in Minnesota where I had never been before

"I'm much happier now"

college girl

"This is the best thing to happen to me since I was five"

college girl

"This is the best moment of my life"

college guy

"Oh my gosh, you make everyone so happy"

college girl named Claire

"You just made my night a lot easier"

a mom

"You're the happiest guy I know who drives an ice cream truck"

teenaged boy at Parmalee Park

"Thank you my good sir"

12-year-old boy

"That's the best thing I've ever seen"

college man to his friend as I drove by at 12:50 a.m. near O.S.U.

"We don't like fancy"

Amish man over 60

"Is zat right !?"

many Amish men after I tell them about my adventures

"I want chocolate"

several young children

One stop involved a 6-year-old boy purchasing a Cherry Chill Cup which is 12 ounces of cherry-flavored frozen fruit punch. He sat down a few feet from the truck to begin enjoying his purchase while I was serving another customer, and then said to me:

"This is good; whuh'ju put in here ?"

I noticed a six-year-old boy running along as if he wanted my attention, but not in the usual way like someone buying ice cream. After returning from a short loop in his neighborhood, he continued his behavior in sync with my driving and then I heard him say to another boy,

"I'm gonna follow him 'til I get my ice cream"

a six-year-old boy bought a Bomb Pop Jr., an older kid who was his neighbor was deciding what to get when the younger kid told him,

"Get this Dude; IT'S FRICKIN SWEEET !!"

One day while driving around, a young girl about age four, ran to her driveway while I was approaching it. She then stood there and waved as I got close. I slowed down because I wondered if she was going to want me to stop. I asked her, "Are you getting ice cream ?" She replied,

"I don't have any money, but, but this is a cool truck. I like your hat"

"I don't like spiders, but I like your hat; it's so October"

college girl named Darcy Phillips. She told me her name after I told her how much I liked her quote and that I wanted to use it.

One of the ice cream sandwiches available on the truck has the three flavors: chocolate, strawberry and vanilla. It is named **Neapolitan.**

Many people who want that item refer to it as the **"Napoleon".** Someone called it, **"Nepa-tea-leon"** Someone else called it **"Napa-lation"**

Another phrase I heard many times by someone talking on a cellular telephone was **"I'm by the ice cream truck"**

I primarily heard that at night near the college crowds while friends were trying to find each other.

"You're a genius"

Many people after dusk who were impressed by my sales strategy.

Many people of various ages, places, and situations have said to me,

"I ain't got no money"

The recurrence of that phrase inspired me to create a poem which focused on that financial situation. I used other phrases or scenarios which I had experienced to come up with: *"Ain't Got No Money"*

Since I wrote it from the perspective of other people, I shot the video the same way. I asked relatives, friends, regular customers and a couple other people if they wanted to be in my video. They loved the idea. It's on Youtube. To see it, search "Ain't got no money for the ice cream truck"

A young girl whose first language is Spanish said to me,

"I have money no"

After serving ice cream to an Amish family, I sat there as the dad and three kids (two girls, and one boy about age three) walked behind me to return to their house with their ice cream. As I put the truck in gear to drive away, the boy looked back at me, and in his sweet little voice with the smallest hint of Dutch accent, said,

"Thank you"

While driving through a very small rural community several counties from Toledo, I was stopped by a 5-year-old girl who said,

"I didn't know the ice cream truck was real; where did you come from ?"

I replied, "Toledo"

I doubt that she was familiar with the existence of a city named Toledo, Ohio.

I wondered if she then thought of Toledo as a magical place, a place where ice cream trucks exist, where ice cream trucks are real. They venture from Toledo to bring joy and happiness to the people of the world.

I have learned that the arrival of an ice cream truck causes some people to be speechless. It causes some people to be excited beyond their own comprehension. It causes joy; it causes happiness; it causes thoughts of a better world. It gives people hope of its return.

It gives people hope of another moment filled with fun and smiles.

Those smiles often last long after the truck is gone.

To enjoy many more photos and videos of my ice cream truck adventures, please "LIKE" my facebook page: "Lessons from an Ice Cream Truck"

CPSIA information can be obtained
at www.ICGtesting.com
Printed in the USA
LVOW01s1205290116

472238LV00006B/36/P

9 781478 732013